COMMUNICATION SKILLS
FOR THE WORLD
OF WORK

COMMUNICATION SKILLS FOR THE WORLD OF WORK

Thomas Cheesebro
Linda O'Connor
Francisco Rios

Waukesha County Technical College

Prentice Hall, Englewood Cliffs, NJ 07632

Library of Congress Cataloging-in-Publication Data

Cheesebro, Thomas,
   Communication skills for the world of work / Thomas Cheesebro,
Linda O'Connor, Francisco Rios.
    p. cm.
   ISBN 0-13-155250-3
   1. Communication. 2. O'Connor, Linda,   . 3. Rios,
Francisco,   . I. Title.
P90.C515 1990
302.2—dc20   89-23057
                                      CIP

Editorial/production supervision and
  interior design: **Janet M. DiBlasi**
Cover design: **Maureen Eide**
Manufacturing buyer: **Mary Ann Gloriande**

 © 1990 by Prentice-Hall, Inc.
A Division of Simon & Schuster
Englewood Cliffs, New Jersey 07632

Printed in the United States of America
10 9 8 7 6 5 4 3 2 1

ISBN   0-13-155250-3

Prentice-Hall International (UK) Limited, *London*
Prentice-Hall of Australia Pty. Limited, *Sydney*
Prentice-Hall Canada Inc., *Toronto*
Prentice-Hall Hispanoamericana, S.A., *Mexico*
Prentice-Hall of India Private Limited, *New Delhi*
Prentice-Hall of Japan, Inc., *Tokyo*
Simon & Schuster Asia Pte. Ltd., *Singapore*
Editora Prentice-Hall do Brasil, Ltda., *Rio de Janeiro*

To our spouses,
Deb, Leigh, and Ron

CONTENTS

Chapter 3

SENDING SKILLS   43

Chapter 4

WRITING SKILLS   93

Chapter 5

EMPLOYABILITY SKILLS   121

PREFACE

Communication Skills for the World of Work is designed to provide readers with the necessary skills to secure and maintain satisfying careers in industrial, business, and service occupations.

The text begins with an overview of the communication process. It explains the essentials of effective listening, sending, writing, and employment skills.

Two unique features enhance the usefulness of this text. First, practical applications are emphasized while theoretical information is kept to a minimum so that readers learn through "hands-on" experience. Second, examples and exercises relate directly to everyday situations in the world of work.

We believe that the readers who study the concepts and practice the skills presented in this text will be more successful in interpersonal relationships, both on and off the job.

ACKNOWLEDGMENTS

We would like to thank the following individuals for their contributions to this text: Deb Stern, Beth McDonald, and Deb Wenzel for word processing; Deb Stern and Jeani Schultz for illustrations; Jim Schroeder and Leigh Barker for their help in editing and revising; and the entire staff and faculty of the Communication Skills Department at Waukesha County Technical College for their feedback and support.

A special thanks to Deb, Leigh, and Ron (our spouses) for their encouragement and patience throughout this endeavor.

Thomas Cheesebro
Linda O'Connor
Francisco Rios

Chapter 1

INTRODUCTION

These questions are designed to stimulate your thinking about the chapter information that follows. Answer these questions on the basis of your own past and present experiences.

1. Define human communication as you understand it. Be as complete as possible.

2. What is the difference between effective communication and ineffective communication?

3. Reflecting on your own experience of relating and interacting with others, list some major principles (comprehensive and fundamental laws, doctrines, assumptions and/or rules) about communication.

4. Why do people communicate? What needs are met?

5. List your own communication strengths and weaknesses.

—————— Ineffective Communication: a Dialogue ————————————————

Pat and Chris sit talking before class about their new schedule this semester:

PAT: What classes do you have this semester?

CHRIS: Well, I have welding, fluid power, machine maintenance, and communications.

PAT: Yeah, I have a communications class too, along with office procedures, data processing, and . . .

CHRIS: I don't see why we have to take communications class. I hate it when they make us take classes.

PAT: I know what you mean. Put a computer in front of me, and I'll communicate with it. Besides, working on computers and things doesn't require that you talk to anyone.

CHRIS: Communication teachers probably have you do lip and tongue exercises. I sure wish I knew why they make you take this class. I communicate well with others. Just last night I . . .

PAT: Hey, did you see the basketball game last night?

CHRIS: Quit interrupting me; you rude slob. I was saying something, and you cut right in. You weren't even listening.

PAT: I'm not rude. You're just a grease monkey. And I'm not a slob. I bought these clothes from . . .

CHRIS: The Salvation Army. I'm greasy because I work with machines all day, not like some people who just tinker with typewriters. Anyone can do that!

PAT: Oh yeah? Well, just try to fix your resume someday; you'll find out it's not that easy.

CHRIS: Well, at least I'd rather wreck something myself than leave it in the hands of an incompetent.

PAT: You're calling me incompetent. I'm not sure I like you.

CHRIS: And you're the epitome of the scum of the earth.

PAT: I should punch your lights out, but instead I'm going to class. I hope I never see you again.

CHRIS: That would be a dream too beautiful to be real. Go on, get out of here. All this got started because of that stupid class I have to take which is useless. I don't need a communications class; you do! I communicate fine. Just ask my mother.

Pat and Chris communicated, but did they communicate effectively? What is communication? Have you ever stopped to define it? Does anyone really know how it works? Why do we communicate?

Additionally, how does the study of communication affect you in your pursuit of a career or with relationships that you already have? Finally, what are some major rules and laws which govern our communication with others?

We will explore these important questions throughout this text. They are tough questions with even tougher answers. But these are also necessary questions which must be dealt with because they affect our ability to get along with others as we attempt to make a valuable contribution to society through employment.

By studying effective communication, we can find new and perhaps better ways of dealing with those people who are important in our lives: those people we work with, learn with, and live with.

This chapter will define communication, list reasons why we interact with others, suggest major principles, develop a model of the communication process, and conclude with a description of some important human characteristics that are essential for effective communication.

Communication Defined

What is communication? This is the first question we must answer before we undertake the study of it. Obviously, communication means different things to different people. To the supervisor on a job, it is a way of making sure that the job gets done. To those who love us, it is a way of maintaining that relationship. To friends and co-workers, it is the tool that helps us to get along.

Communication is sometimes defined as the process of sending and receiving messages. When a customer explains a problem to you about the exhaust system of a car, a message has been sent, and you have, supposedly, received it.

What if the language use, however, is not clear? For example, if the customer says, "Every time I'm driving, my car makes funny noises, and smoke comes from that thing in the back and from that little jobber over yonder."

A message has been sent, and you have received it. Communication, as defined above, has taken place. But you still don't know what's wrong with the car or how the customer wants it fixed. This suggests that more needs to happen for communication to be effective. For one thing, the customer needs to be more specific in describing the problem. You need to listen carefully and ask clarifying questions. The goal is to achieve shared understanding of the information being sent.

In addition, effective communication involves more than just understanding the information. It involves the shared understanding of the feelings, thoughts, wants, needs, and intentions of the communicators, which may not be openly expressed in words.

Note that shared understanding and agreeing with someone are two different things. For example, I may not agree with my boss on the correct way to file customer accounts, but I can still try to understand her way, even in my disagreement.

Why Do We Communicate?

People communicate for a number of important reasons: to meet practical needs, to fulfill social needs, to make better decisions, and to promote personal growth.

Practical Functions

We communicate in order to have practical needs met, such as buying food, renting an apartment, securing a job, and maintaining our health and safety. Travelers to foreign countries know how difficult it is to have these needs met when they do not speak the language.

Social Functions

We often communicate with others for the sheer pleasure of interaction. Communication also enables us to meet others, demonstrate ties, maintain friendships, and build intimate relationships.

Are our social needs important? Failure to meet our social needs often results in serious consequences: loneliness, loss of job productivity, drug and alcohol abuse, marital problems, divorce, and even suicide. We all need to have the affection of others, to feel like we belong, and to exercise control over our lives.

Decision Making Functions

Communication can and should help us to make decisions about our own lives. Generally the more information we receive, the better decisions we make.

Let's say, for example, that the radio alarm clock goes off and you hear, "Good morning. It's 6 a.m. Sam Sunshine here. Rise and shine. It's 60 degrees out and clear." With this little bit of information, you can decide how much longer you can stay in bed, whether to wear your overcoat or windbreaker, and whether you'll "bike" it or take the old "clunker" to school.

Not all decisions are this simple. We use information to decide what job to take, where to live, and who to marry.

Communication serves a
decision-making function.

Personal Growth Functions

Communication can also be seen as the primary means of intellectual, emotional, social, and psychological growth. Through self-expression and feedback from others, we define and confirm who we are, feel appreciated and successful, obtain new information, increase our level of awareness, and expose ourselves to challenging new experiences. As a result, we grow as people.

_____ Principles of Communication _____

Growth through communication can happen when we understand some of the major "principles" of human interaction; that is, some important rules, laws, doctrines, or assumptions about communication.

1. We are always communicating, whether we intend to or not. Try to stop communicating. What would you do? Leave? Sleep? Go into a corner and put headphones on? If nothing else, you'd communicate a desire not to communicate. It has been found that 75 percent of our waking day is

spent communicating through reading, writing, speaking, and listening. This figure, however, does not include the amount of time we talk to ourselves (either silently or out loud).

2. The message sent is not necessarily the same message received. In fact, 50 percent of our daily communication is misunderstood. While we are sharing information important to us, others spend half of the time dozing off, thinking of something else, or simply misinterpreting what we have said.

3. A part of the message is who sends it. It is impossible to divorce a message from who sends it. Assume, for example, you hear the message, "I love you." Would the meaning of the message change if it were said by a stranger, spouse, friend, or enemy? Of course it would.

4. The meanings of words are inside of us. Words don't mean—people attach meaning to words. When Farmer Fred and Biker Bob talk about their new "hogs," there's a good chance they mean different "animals."

5. Communication is learned. We learn the language, gestures, and customs of the culture we are brought up in. Because of this, communication is "culture bound."

Different cultures communicate differently. Eskimos have 25 different words for "snow" and no words for war. Arabs communicate at such a close distance as to make most Americans feel uncomfortable.

Greeting an acquaintance with a handshake is acceptable in the U.S. but may seem to others as a cold and impersonal way to say hello. For them, a hug and kiss on the cheek would be more appropriate, even with members of the same sex.

Since most communication is learned, we can learn ineffective ways of communicating, but we can also relearn new and sometimes better ways.

The Process of Communication

One way to see how communication works is to examine a process model. A process model for communication is much like a schematic for an electrical appliance. They both show the internal workings of a complex process in a simplified way. A communication process model breaks communication down into its separate parts and puts it onto a two-dimensional surface for inspection. An interpersonal model of communication might look like the figure on page 7.

Sender/Receiver

The first component of communication is the sender/receiver. Though we separate these two tasks, it is important to keep in mind that we do both at the same time. While speaking to you, I receive nonverbal feedback on what I am saying. Because of this, people act as "transceivers," a combination of transmitters (senders) and receivers.

More specifically, the sender originates a communication message. An idea comes into mind, and an attempt is made to put this thought into symbols (nonverbal gestures or verbal language) that the receiver will understand. This process of changing thought into symbols is called *encoding*.

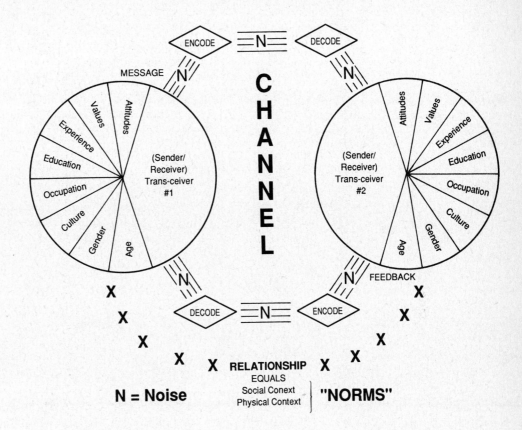

ENVIRONMENT = Physical Context

N = Noise

RELATIONSHIP
EQUALS
Social Conext
Physical Context

"NORMS"

The receiver, who is the destination of the communication message, must assign meaning to the symbols so they can be understood. This process of assigning meaning is called *decoding*, and like encoding, it happens so fast, we rarely think about it. We simply assume we understand what the symbols mean.

Each person, sender and receiver, is a product of experiences, feelings, gender (male/female), occupation, religion, values, mood, etc. As a result, each person is unique and, therefore, each person's encoding and decoding is unique. I could tell you that I am a successful secretary and mean that I'm satisfied with my work. You may think that this means I make a good salary.

Message

The message is the idea, thought, feeling, or opinion to be communicated. Sometimes the message is clear and direct; for example, when I tell you to get me a package of disks for the microprocessor.

Other times the message is unclear, as when a job interviewer says, "We'll keep your application on file." Does this mean you'll be called for the next vacancy, or is this a polite way of saying you're not qualified, and you'll never hear from the employer again?

At all times, we are sending several messages simultaneously. Along with the actual content of a message, a speaker may be sending a feeling message which suggests how that speaker feels about the content and the relationship. These feeling messages are usually communicated nonverbally or vocally.

Channel

The channel is the line through which the message travels from sender to receiver. In face to face communication, messages are carried via stimulated air waves and light waves. Channels can be extended through telephone, television, radio, and newspapers.

Though we use sound and light primarily, people can and do use any sensory channel. How a person smells communicates, as does how firmly a person shakes hands.

Feedback

Feedback is the receiver's response to the message and indicates how the message is seen, heard and understood, and often how the receiver feels about the message and/or the sender. Feedback is an essential component of the communication process and makes communication a two person affair.

In interpersonal relationships where effective communication is the goal, we will want to stimulate as much feedback as possible. In short, feedback is the primary means of increasing personal awareness. We should give and get as much feedback as possible.

Context

Two factors affect what we say and how we say something—the social and the physical context. The social context deals with the relationship between sender and receiver.

Obviously, what you say and how you say it will change, depending upon whether you're talking to your best friend, a total stranger, your boss, Reverend Rivera from your church, or Officer O'Malley of the police department. Also, the physical context will dictate what you say and how you say it. Your communication will change if you're at the local disco, at work, at home, or in church.

The context of communication determines the rules or norms for that interaction. These unwritten, expected ways of behaving vary from situation to situation. Their violation can result in negative consequences. For example, using foul language in a job interview may keep you from getting the job you want. No one is forced to adhere to expected standards, but society does make you bear the consequences for breaking its norms.

Noise

Noise is any interference that prevents shared understanding. Basically there are three types of noise which help create communication breakdowns. These types of noise are internal, external, and semantic.

Internal noise includes our attitudes, opinions, and beliefs toward what is being said, as well as who is saying it, and may inhibit our understanding of others. Our intrapersonal communication (the dialogues which occur inside our heads) can also be a source of disruptive internal noise.

Internal noise is also affected by our self-concept, how we feel and what we expect. If my fiancé told me before class that the wedding was off, I would have a difficult time listening to the lecture because of the noise inside my head dealing with this break up. Daydreaming is the most obvious form of internal noise interfering with communication.

External noise deals with the noise in the environment: other voices, airplanes overhead, buzzing of machines, etc.; it most often affects our interpersonal communication—our communication between people which is "personal." This type of noise is more obvious than internal noise, and is easier to cope with. We cope with this type of noise by tuning it out, turning it off, or speaking up. Most families who live near airports or train stations become extremely good at ignoring external noise even when it shakes and rattles their windows.

Semantic noise, the third type of noise, occurs when sender and receiver have different meanings for the words and/or gestures they use. Semantic noise often occurs when technicians and lay people talk to each other. When a printer tells the customer he'll burn an image of the customer's picture, the printer means he'll create a copy while the customer may assume his picture will be torched and destroyed.

Other Elements of Effective Communication

The next three chapters will focus on essential "skills" of effective communication. These are the "tools" of communication. As such, they can be used positively to build stronger relationships, to enhance job satisfaction, and to reduce misunderstandings.

The presentation of these skills is based on four assumptions about your attitudes toward human relations:

1. You are capable of accepting other people for who they are, regardless of race, attitudes, or behavior. *(unconditional positive regard)*

2. You are capable of having an interest in other people and of wanting to know about their feelings, thoughts, and experiences by putting yourself in their shoes and understanding their viewpoint through active listening. *(empathy)*

3. You are capable of communicating with others and sharing your own feelings, thoughts, and experiences. *(openness)*

4. You are capable of being honest and true about who you are and how you feel. *(congruence)*

These four ingredients are communication essentials and make all the skills worthwhile and valuable.

CHAPTER 1 CHECK UP

Use these key words from the preceding chapter to complete the following sentences.

sender	✓transceiver	interpersonal
receiver	✓message	external
noise	✓decoding	✓encoding
channel	✓internal	✓social function
✓communication	✓intrapersonal	✓semantic

1. The communication inside our heads is called *intrapersonal*

2. The process of turning our thoughts into symbols is *encoding*.

3. *transceiver* is the idea that we are both sender and receiver while we communicate.

4. The process of assigning meanings to words and gestures we receive is called *decoding*

5. When I have understood "completely" what was said, as the sender intended it to be understood, we have completed effective *communication*.

6. The idea, thought, or feeling conveyed is called the *message*.

7. The sender sends a message through a *channel* to the receiver.

8. Daydreaming is a type of *internal* noise.

9. Communication helps us to make decisions, but we also communicate with others because it fulfills a *social function*.

10. *Semantic* noise is that which is created by misinterpretation of symbols (words and gestures).

1. verbal
2. nonverbal (Body lang.)
3. written

FEEDBACK EXERCISE

This exercise will help you discover the importance of feedback as it relates to "understanding" what is being communicated. Your instructor will describe three different diagrams to you. In each instance you are to draw, as accurately as possible, the diagram as it is explained. In all three situations, note how much time it took to draw the diagram (Time), how sure you were that you matched the original (Confidence Level), and how closely your drawing resembled the sender's (Accuracy).

Situation 1: there should be no verbal or nonverbal feedback from the audience.

Situation 2: there should be nonverbal but *no* verbal feedback from the audience.

Situation 3: use *as much* feedback as possible.

DIAGRAM 1	**DIAGRAM 2**	**DIAGRAM 3**
Accuracy _____	Accuracy _____	Accuracy _____
Confidence Level _____	Confidence Level _____	Confidence Level _____
Time _____	Time _____	Time _____

QUESTIONS

1. Which diagram took longest explaining? Shortest? Why?

2. Which diagram was most frustrating to listen to?

3. Which diagram had the highest degree of accuracy?

4. How did your confidence level differ throughout the three diagrams?

5. What conclusions can you draw from this experiment about the role of feedback in communication?

PERSONAL EXPERIENCE TALK

The purpose of this exercise is to give you the opportunity to speak in front of the class. The goal is to increase your confidence in speaking before groups. You are asked to share a personal experience from your life and explain the lesson you learned from that experience.

The guidelines for this speech experience are as follows:

1. Choose a personal experience that was meaningful and true. The talk may be serious or humorous. The experience you share should also be one you feel will be of interest to the class.
2. Be sure to share all the necessary details of the experience by including answers to the questions of who, what, where, when, and why. Create a storytelling atmosphere by using specific and vivid language.
3. Finish your talk with a short and clear statement about what you learned from the experience.
4. The amount of time suggested for this presentation is between two and three minutes.
5. Practice the speech several times before the actual classroom presentation. Practice in front of a friend and ask for some suggestions for improvement.
6. Use the space provided for notes. You are encouraged, however, to speak extemporaneously—carefully prepared but delivered without notes.

EXPERIENCE:

Who, Where, When, What, Why.

LESSON LEARNED:

COMMUNICATION SURVEY

This survey is intended to give you an opportunity to see your strengths and weaknesses as they relate to your communication abilities. This survey is not going to be used by any person other than yourself, so you should be honest in answering the questions. When completed, this survey will give you some idea of which areas you may want to pay particular attention to as you proceed through the course.

Scoring should be based on the following scale:

3 points = a definite strength
2 points = an area I would like to improve
1 point = a definite weakness

_____ 1. Listen completely and attentively without distraction.

_____ 2. Respond to others in a way that shows you were listening to them.

_____ 3. Detect main ideas and their supporting points.

_____ 4. Use clarifying questions to promote understanding.

_____ 5. Summarize directions, statements, or feelings shared with you by others.

_____ 6. Spell and define technical terms as they relate to your job specialty.

_____ 7. Talk freely and confidently to employers about your favorable qualities in a job interview.

_____ 8. Clearly state important information about work experiences, educational experiences, and personal qualities on a résumé.

_____ 9. Fill out applications for employment accurately, neatly, and completely.

_____ 10. Write and send business letters regarding employment.

_____ 11. Give instructions to others which are clear, concise, and direct.

_____ 12. Express feelings to others at work and at home.

_____ 13. Separate fact from opinion.

_____ 14. Skillfully discuss differences of opinion with others.

_____ 15. Employ successful problem-solving techniques when faced with a conflict.

_____ 16. Choose specific words to communicate your ideas in writing.

_____ 17. Write a clear, accurate set of directions.

_____ 18. Draft letters and memos that are free of wordiness and extra information.

_____ **19.** Write logically organized ideas.

_____ **20.** Verify factual information included in your writing.

COMMUNICATION SURVEY SCORING KEY

Use the following scoring key to assess your perceived ability to communicate. When finished scoring, answer the questions which follow.

LISTENING SKILL	EMPLOYABILITY SKILL	SPEAKING SKILL	WRITING SKILL
Questions 1–5	Questions 6–10	Questions 11–15	Questions 16–20

Total _____   _____   _____   _____

	SCORING	TOTAL
	No perceived problem with these communication skills.	11–15
	Need work to improve these skills.	6–10
	Need maximum efforts to develop communication strengths.	5

1. What do the results of this survey tell you about your ability to communicate?

2. How close do these results compare to your own personal assessment of your communication ability?

3. In what areas do you need special improvement? How might you go about improving your ability in these areas?

Chapter 2

LISTENING SKILLS

───── Preview Questions ─────────────────────────

These questions are designed to stimulate your thinking about the chapter information that follows. Answer these questions on the basis of your past and present experiences.

1. Define listening. Be specific. How does it differ from hearing?

2. How would you rate your listening skills on a scale of 1 to 10 (with 10 being excellent and 1 poor)? Why? How would your employers and family members rate your listening skills?

3. What are some of your reasons for not listening?

4. How do you feel when you're not being listened to?

5. How do you know if someone is listening to you?

6. What specific listening skills/techniques do you use which help you to listen effectively when you really have to?

7. How do you respond to people who share a problem with you? How do you want others to respond to you when you share a problem?

8. In what ways does your ability to listen harm/help your job performance?

——— Poor Listening: a Dialogue ————————————————————

Mario and Jan sit talking in the school cafeteria:

MARIO: How's that math class going for you this semester? I hear it's really
         a tough course.

  JAN: The class is not half as bad as the other things that have been
         happening in my life lately *(sighs)*.

MARIO: I know what you mean . . . My girlfriend and I have been mad at each
         other for the last several weeks, and I'm too proud to tell her how
         much I enjoy her when she's around.

  JAN: My family's farm is about to be foreclosed on, and we just don't know
         what we're going to do.

MARIO: She called me up the other day to ask me how I was doing, but I just
         acted like I wasn't even interested in talking to her.

  JAN: I just wonder if my coming to school didn't have something to do
         with it. I mean, I could've gotten a job or something.

MARIO: After she hung up, I knew that I had blown it. I just didn't know what
         to say to her.

  JAN: I also have to think that if I'd worked a little harder and had more
         knowledge of farming we could have been more independent.

MARIO: I'm thinking about calling her up and. . . .

  JAN: I just think that if I'd been a little luckier and had more cooperation
         from the weather, it might have worked. But there was so much snow
         on the ground earlier this fall that no one but skiers were happy.

MARIO: That's it! I'll call her up and ask her if she wants to go skiing. That's
         something we both like to do, and it will give us a chance to talk
         things out. I'll probably have to hit up my dad for a loan to pull it off.

  JAN: Maybe a loan is the answer. It could hold off the sale temporarily, and
         before the loan comes due, I'll have a job. It's worth a chance. Hey,
         you know, it was really nice talking with you.

MARIO: I know what you mean. It's so easy to find a person who will lend an ear like you did. But we have to go to communications class. Can you believe it? The class is going to be studying listening this week! Maybe we can test out!

JAN: I did test out of that welding class, so maybe I won't have that much longer to go. Then I can. . . .

Fortunately, not everybody listens as badly as Mario and Jan. But how well do you listen? Do you comprehend fully what you are being told by supervisors, teachers, friends, and family? How would they rate your listening skills, or lack of them? In what kinds of situations do you find it most difficult to listen? Finally, how do you respond to others who attempt to share their personal or occupational concerns with you?

All of these are important questions that need to be addressed. When one considers the time and money that is spent correcting errors because somebody didn't listen properly, it's no wonder that employers rate listening as a communication essential.

Furthermore, the hurt feelings generated when we fail to actively demonstrate our listening skills can damage our personal and occupational relationships with others. People may be fired, customers lost, and working relationships strained because of ineffective listening. Likewise, friendships suffer, marriages fail, and families grow apart when individuals fail to listen with genuine concern.

No doubt, the importance of listening seems self-evident. In fact, on the average we spend nearly half of our communication time listening. Yet studies suggest that we are mediocre listeners at best. Estimates of listening efficiency hover around 25 percent, meaning that we generally will miss three-quarters of what we hear.

The goal of this chapter is to explore bad listening habits, discover effective alternative behaviors, and develop responding skills that promote understanding.

Bad Listening: Some Problems

There are many reasons why we don't listen very effectively. Listening problems can be grouped into five general categories: lack of specific training, message overload, yielding to distractions, losing emotional control, and failing to use the thought-speed advantage.

One explanation for poor listening abilities is that most of us have not been taught how to listen. Throughout our formal education, we are offered courses in reading, writing, and speaking, but rarely are we offered training in listening skills. Certainly we learned how to listen as we watched and imitated those around us whom we admired: parents, family, and friends. But they, like most of those untrained in listening, probably were only mediocre listeners themselves.

Another factor which contributes to poor listening is the mistaken belief that because we are bombarded with an overwhelming number of messages daily, we somehow learn to listen automatically. Radio commercials scream at us when we drive to work; machines grind, whir, and hum the noises of production; a barrage of chatter deafeningly echoes as we sit in the student center reviewing for an upcoming exam; stereo systems "whoof and tweet" us into oblivion with nonstop rock. Such an overload, instead of helping us to listen better, teaches us to tune out many of the messages we receive.

Even when we choose to listen, we are influenced by external and internal distractions. Problems occur when we choose to focus our attention on these distractions instead of on the speaker's message. Examples of external distractions, as mentioned above, constantly compete for our attention and may be both visual and verbal.

We may also tune out a speaker because of distractions that exist inside of our head (internal noise). When we doubt what the speaker is saying, or when we begin to formulate a response before the speaker has concluded, or when we are preoccupied with our own personal problems, internal distractions keep us from listening well.

Losing emotional control is a fourth listening problem. Our listening effectiveness drops as our emotional response increases. Listening while you are experiencing intense anger, happiness, or boredom is very difficult.

Sometimes the emotional reaction is directly related to what the speaker is saying or how it is being said. For example, listening to a pro-union speaker when you are strongly against collective representation is difficult because such opinions oppose your attitudes, values, and beliefs.

Likewise, if the speaker begins labeling those who express anti-union beliefs as "scabs," chances are your listening effectiveness will drop to zero. Emotional control, though not easy to achieve, is essential for successful listening.

Finally, failing to use the thought-speed advantage is a major source of our listening problems. Because we can think so much faster than anyone can

Listening while experiencing
intense emotion is very difficult.

talk, we often fool ourselves by believing that we can take mental holidays, daydream, plan, or worry and still listen at the same time.

The fact is that the more we allow our minds to wander, the stronger this tendency to tune out the speaker becomes. The result might be sitting in a lecture on business math and not hearing a word the speaker is saying.

By no means are these the only reasons why we don't listen well, but they constitute the bulk of our listening problems. In any case, the first step to solving a problem is to become aware of it; you must find out what causes your bad listening habits and take steps to overcome them. Unfortunately, these poor listening patterns may come from well established habits. Fortunately, these listening problems can be improved if we learn new and better habits to replace the old ones.

Effective Listening: Some Suggestions

While many suggestions are offered to help us become better listeners, real improvement requires a caring attitude and attentive, responsive behavior. The central attitude important to listening effectively is "I *want* to understand you." Until you make this decision as a conscious choice, you will be easily distracted from the important listening task at hand. This attitude is rooted in wanting to know about others: their experiences, perceptions, and feelings while withholding any judgments of the speaker.

Until we go beyond our own personal preoccupations and focus our concentration on the speaker, effective listening will be haphazard at best.

After we've made the decision to really listen, proper attending behavior is an initial skill that the listener needs to use. Attending behaviors are a combination of the attitude already mentioned and actions which communicate involvement with the speaker and demonstrate interest and concern. Equally important, this caring attitude and attentive behavior keep the listener involved in the listening process, focus the listener's attention on the speaker, and reduce both external and internal distractions.

Actions associated with good attending behavior include eye contact that is appropriate in duration, frequency, and intensity; body posture that reflects your interest and involvement; and interpersonal distance that is suitable for the message being shared.

Each of these three components has a best or optimum level of effectiveness. The good listener uses an appropriate amount of eye contact, an attentive body posture, and a comfortable interpersonal distance (See the figure on page 23).

Good attending behavior that shows caring, strengthens the relationship and sets the stage for effective listening.

Finally, we offer the following suggestions:

1. *Stop talking*—you can't listen and talk at the same time.
2. *Hear the speaker out*—wait until the speaker has completed the message before offering a response of your own.
3. *Tune out distractions*—eliminate distractions whenever possible, and practice good attending behavior to minimize distractions which can't be eliminated.

... and then he told me that he was unsure about our relationship and needed time to be apart.

Hmm. Good eye contact. Good posture. Comfortable distance. Now she thinks I'm listening. Which movie shall I go to tonight.

Actions and attitudes keep the listener involved in the listening process.

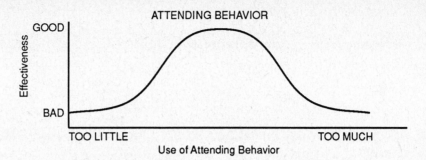

4. *Don't lose your cool*—develop an open-minded tolerance for ideas and opinions different from your own; learn which loaded words produce strong emotional reactions for you; and stop mentally debating with the speaker before you fully understand what is being said.

5. *Take advantage of thought-speed*—review what the speaker has said; relate the message to your own past experiences and present knowledge; and anticipate the speaker's next line of thought.

Certainly this list is not complete, but it is a start. Now it's up to you to identify the listening problems that affect you the most and find ways to overcome these problems.

RESPONSE STYLE QUESTIONNAIRE

Read each of the twelve situations listed next, and write a response that is typical of what you would normally say as a listener. Then go back, and read the sample responses for each situation. Circle the sample that most closely resembles the intention of the response you've written, even though the wording may be different. If there are no matches, circle the one that sounds like something you might say in response to the problem.

1. The union just told us we have to take another five point cut in pay because the company is in bad economic straits. I don't know what I'm going to do. With a family of three kids to support, it will be hard making ends meet.
   Your Response:

   a. You have no right to complain. Just be thankful you've got a job.
   b. I know what you mean. My company cut back on our vacation time because of financial problems.
   c. It sounds like you're feeling depressed about that salary loss.
   d. You may be concerned because you've never been forced to budget your money before, and you're not sure how to go about it.
   e. How much was the other cut you had to take?

2. I'm seriously thinking about the boss' offer to have the company send me to school part-time to upgrade my skills. But I don't know—I was never much of a student in high school; I don't know if I've got what it takes to go on to a technical school.
   Your Response:

   a. What do you mean when you say you weren't much of a student in high school?
   b. You're having doubts about your ability to succeed in school?
   c. You'll be sorry if you don't take the boss up on this offer, especially since the company agreed to pay for it.
   d. Most people have apprehensions about returning to school. But you can make it!
   e. Perhaps you're worried about being embarrassed in front of the boss if you don't get all A's and B's.

3. Kelly, my partner who works next to me in the shop, has really been depressed lately, and it's starting to affect the quality of our work. I'd like to say something, but I'm afraid I'll just be butting in.
   Your Response:

   a. Everyone seems to go through periods of depression like that. Just give it time; I'm sure it'll blow over.
   b. Has Kelly given you any hints about what might be wrong?
   c. It could be that Kelly is still feeling bad about not getting that promotion last month.
   d. If I were you, I'd mind my own business. Wait until Kelly is ready to talk about it.
   e. It seems as if you want to help Kelly without appearing nosy.

4. I'm really having a hard time getting along with the new supervisor. He's the company owner's son, and he seems to feel he can push everybody around because his mom owns the business.
   Your Response:

   a. How has he been pushing you around?
   b. If I were you, I'd go and complain to the owner about it.
   c. I get the idea you're unhappy with the way this supervisor is handling the people in your department.
   d. It could be that he feels the need to prove his supervisory ability to his mother.
   e. If you can just hang in there a little longer, the situation is bound to improve.

5. I just can't talk to my parents anymore since I told them Terry and I are getting married. They are always asking questions about where I go and what I do. They keep track of me like I am a two-year-old. I don't know what has happened to them.
   Your Response:

   a. Why don't you tell them to butt out? They shouldn't be hassling you.
   b. What do they want to know?
   c. You sound really upset about this.
   d. They're probably just finding it hard to let go of you now that you're getting married.
   e. Lots of parents are like that all the time. I'm sure it will pass.

6. Lupe, I hate it when those customers call and say their appliances conked out on them after we just fixed them. Half of the people barely know how to plug them in, much less run them. Then I get stuck listening to all their problems on the phone.
   Your Response:

   a. They really do get you upset, don't they?
   b. What was wrong with that last caller?
   c. Just tell them to read their owner's manual.

    d. Sometimes they worry more about something when it's new or fixed. That's why they call so much.

    e. I had the same grief when I had your job; you'll get used to it.

7. The crew on the line keep inviting me to join them at a bar after work. I feel obligated to go, being the new employee and all. Sometimes I can't afford to buy a round, but everybody usually buys one. I hate to be rude, so what do I do?

    Your Response:

    a. Don't go just because you feel obligated. That's dumb.

    b. Perhaps you think you need to do this to feel accepted by them.

    c. So you're worried about fitting in with the crew on the assembly line, but you're not sure you can afford being one of the group.

    d. Where do you usually go anyway?

    e. I was in the same situation at the last place I worked. I guess it's the normal thing to do when you're new on your first job.

8. I really like working here. The opportunities are great; the conditions are excellent; the pay is good. I've learned a lot. But Kerry, that perfectionist boss we have . . . I just can't seem to do enough right. There's always something wrong with the work I've done.

    Your Response:

    a. Hey, you'll get through okay. I'm sure Kerry will see that you're working up to your potential.

    b. You think the boss demands too much from you?

    c. Kerry's boss used to treat him the same way. Kerry probably thinks that's what a good boss does.

    d. What did Kerry say to you last night?

    e. If I were you, I'd find something else to do or somebody else to work for.

9. Chris, can I borrow some of your tools? My tools were ripped off from my truck, and that was only one of several bad things that happened this weekend.

    Your Response:

    a. Yeah, those kinds of weekends happen every now and then to all of us.

    b. You can borrow some today, but you'd better get some new tools soon, or you'll get fired.

    c. Sounds like you had a real bad weekend.

    d. Maybe your tools were stolen because you left your doors unlocked again.

    e. Where was your truck parked when your tools got ripped off?

10. My boss is really rude. Three months ago I asked if I could have a vacation in early July and was told yes. I've made all kinds of plans to go out west, and now the boss said that if I go, I'll be fired.
Your Response:

   a. After promising you vacation, your boss has threatened action if you take it?
   b. Why do you think the boss changed so suddenly?
   c. I'd go to a union officer and file a grievance.
   d. A lot of the workers around here feel the same about their boss.
   e. The company must have just gotten a new order in, and now they need your help.

11. It's really hard being the only female in an all male shop. I get teased to death by all the employees who don't think I'm serious about diesel mechanics.
Your Response:

   a. You're being too sensitive about the issue. Just ignore their remarks.
   b. That must really be a hassle. If there's anything I can say or do to help change things, just let me know.
   c. What do they say that is most irritating when they tease you?
   d. You seem fed up with the other employees' comments?
   e. Maybe they're intimidated by a woman in this occupation.

12. It's totally useless! Everywhere I go for jobs, I'm told that nothing is available or that I don't have enough experience. How can I get any experience unless somebody is willing to just give me a chance?
Your Response:

   a. What kind of jobs are you applying for? What are your qualifications?
   b. You want to work, but you lack the needed experience?
   c. You're going about it all wrong. You should go to school and get an advanced education in that area.
   d. The economy is in such a mess that employers have a greater pool of potential workers. They can now afford to be really choosy.
   e. You're only one of many people in the same boat.

—————— Responding Choices ——————————————————————————

In addition to the attitudes and actions already described which promote clear understanding, the listener must choose how to respond to the message received.

The choice of response becomes especially critical when someone shares a personal or professional problem. In such situations, you have an opportunity to respond in several ways. Your response reflects your reaction to the situation as well as your intentions, and may encourage open communication and problem solving or inhibit a further sharing and understanding.

Take a closer look at the choices that are available to you as you react. Does your response help you to listen? Does your response help the person with the problem?

Suppose Shawn, your classmate and friend, comes to you and relates the following:

> "I don't know about this program. I thought I wanted to work in appliance servicing, and now I find out how much electricity and electronics are involved, and I don't know. I hate electronics. Schematics look like puzzles to me. I don't know if I'm going to make it in this program or not."

As you respond to Shawn's problem, you may feel evaluative or judgmental, curious, concerned, analytical, supportive, or empathic. The feelings and reactions that you have can be shared clearly with Shawn if you are aware of the different responses that are available to you.

Research has identified several types of responses. The following is a partial list of common responses that you can chose from as you provide feedback to the concerns of others.

1. *Evaluating (judges, evaluates, advises, or solves).* There are two types of evaluating responses, those that judge and those that advise. Those that judge say what is right or wrong, good or bad. Examples might be: That was stupid! That's right! You're great! That's important!

   Responses that advise offer a solution to the person's problem by telling him what to do. Examples might include these: If I were you I would . . . You really should . . . You ought to . . . Why don't you. . . . An evaluating response to Shawn might be, "You're in over your head. I'd bail out as fast as I can if I were you and go into another program."

2. *Interpreting (interprets, explains, teaches).* This response explains why something happens, or states cause(s) for actions and feelings by adding information not stated in the original problem. Examples might include these: You may feel that way because . . . She probably did that because . . . Maybe the reason this problem came about is due to. . . .

   An interpreting response to Shawn might be, "Maybe you're afraid of burning yourself with the electrical wires because of that time you were burnt while fixing that television."

3. *Supporting (reassures, supports).* Supporting responses attempt to make people feel better, cheer them up, or offer help, encouragement, or comfort. Probably one of the most effective supportive responses is one that states how you are able to help in terms of being available and offering your services, time, or possessions. Examples may be: I'm sure things will be better . . . Look at the progress you have made since . . . We all feel that way once in awhile . . . If there is any way I can help . . . I'd be willing to come over and help you with. . . .

A supporting response to Shawn might be, "I feel that way about school also. If you like, we can work on the homework together for awhile and see how it goes."

4. *Questioning (probes, questions).* Questioning requests more information or clarity of information. There are two types of questions: the "open" question requires more than yes or no answers and encourages greater freedom of response; the "closed" question can be answered with a yes or no. Examples include these: What makes you think that? How long have you felt that way? Where were you . . .? What do you mean by that?

A questioning response to Shawn might be, "How come you're having such a hard time with those classes in particular? What can be done to make you feel more comfortable about taking them?

5. *Paraphrasing (summarizes, restates, reflects).* This response shows what you've understood by restating in your own words what you think the speaker meant or by summarizing the content and/or feelings in the message. Examples might be these: You mean you're feeling . . . So what you are saying is . . . In other words . . . If I understand you've. . . .

A paraphrasing response to Shawn might be, "You're unsure of your own ability in some of the courses and are wondering whether you should just bail out of the program?"

An important point to remember is that these responses are not right or wrong. They all have their place in effective interaction with those who have problems. However, practice is needed by the good listener to develop skillful and appropriate use of these responses.

Now go back to the Response Style Questionnaire and identify each of the responses for each situation. An example of each response is provided for every situation. Then look at the responses you wrote and label them. Record how many of each type of response you've used. Do you have a dominant response style?

Using the Response Styles

Approximately 80 percent of all the feedback we give to senders can be categorized as either evaluating, interpreting, supporting, questioning or paraphrasing responses.

The evaluating response appears to be the one used most frequently when senders share problems with listeners. The frequency of the evaluating response may be the result of listeners feeling responsible to solve senders' problems by offering advice or believing that they (the listeners') know what is in the senders' best interests.

In contrast, paraphrasing tends to be used least often, most likely because it is a response we must be specifically taught to use.

One response is not necessarily better to use than another. Rather, the overuse, underuse, or inappropriate use of any response is what can make feedback ineffective. According to psychologist Carl Rogers, if we use any response 40 percent of the time or more, people tend to see us as always responding that way.

Consequently, if we use a large number of evaluating responses in communication, we may be perceived by others as being judgmental and closed minded individuals, which can lessen our effectiveness as listeners.

Certain guidelines can enable us to use the response styles more effectively. In addition, senders give us some cues to let us know when a particular response is working (i.e., helping the sender deal with a problem). When senders come to us with problems, let us try to keep in mind the following responses.

Evaluating

The evaluating response normally does not help a sender in coping with a problem unless the sender specifically asks for advice. Even if advice is requested by a sender, the listener should feel confident that the sender is ready to accept the advice and is unlikely to blame the listener if the advice does not work out. An indication that advice is working occurs when the sender willingly accepts the advice, almost as if it represents a solution the sender hadn't previously thought of. If the sender openly disagrees with the advice or responds with "Yes, but . . ." and proceeds to explain why the advice won't work, chances are the evaluating response is not being effective.

Interpreting

This response works best when the listener's intention is to offer a sincere analysis of the problem's causes. Interpreting also tends to work more effectively when stated nonabsolutely, such as "Maybe you feel this way because. . ." or "Perhaps you're feeling undecided as a result of. . . ." This nonabsolute language acknowledges that the listener may not be completely accurate in the analysis, and therefore, potential defensive or argumentative reactions in the sender are likely to be reduced. If the sender agrees with your analysis, interpreting is working. If the sender disagrees and proceeds to tell you why you're wrong, interpreting is unsuccessful.

Supporting

Support and reassurance work best when the sender has already determined how to solve the problem and simply needs the strength and encouragement that your support can provide. If this response is working, the sender will accept your words of comfort and assume a more relaxed nonverbal posture; if not, the sender may say something like, "But you don't really understand."

Questioning

When additional information is genuinely needed, questioning works best. If questions are used, ask them one at a time; ask them only as often as necessary; keep them open ended. You may also want to ask questions that make the sender think more deeply about the problem such as, "What might be some underlying causes of this problem?" "How do you feel about this?" "What do you think you can do about this?" If questioning is having the desired effect, the sender will gladly provide the information requested; if not, the sender may begin sharing less.

Paraphrasing

Paraphrasing reveals a genuine desire on the part of a listener to listen nonjudgmentally with full understanding of the sender's thoughts and feelings. The sender can then talk through the problem and arrive at a solution in an atmosphere of acceptance. If paraphrasing is being effective, the sender will continue to share thoughts and feelings in greater depth or correct you if your understanding is inaccurate. If the sender retreats and begins to share less, paraphrasing is probably not being successful.

CHAPTER 2 CHECK UP

Use these key words from the preceding chapter to complete the following sentences.

understanding	losing emotional control	questioning
external noise	internal noise	agreement
evaluating	thought-speed advantage	facts
supporting	paraphrasing	interpreting
attending behavior	"I *want* to understand"	

1. The type of sound made by jackhammers, rock bands, and computer printers that compete for our attention and make it difficult to listen is called _____.

2. A response that states *why* a person's problem exists is called _____.

3. The goal of effective listening is _____.

4. A response that rephrases in your own words the speaker's content and/or feelings is called _____.

5. Good eye contact, forward leaning body posture, and a comfortable distance between you and the speaker are aspects of _____.

6. The response that asks for additional information or clarity of information is called _____.

7. When listening to ourselves while someone is talking to us, we are being distracted by _____.

8. Reviewing, relating, and anticipating are all ways to use _____.

9. A response that tells a sender what "ought" to be done or that offers a judgment is called _____.

10. Making a conscious effort to listen involves the attitude: _____.

INFORMATION PASSING EXERCISE

Imagine that you have been asked to inform a new employee about the responsibilities of his or her job. In a short paragraph of three to five sentences, write an original set of instructions that contains at least five specific details for completing a specific task, such as making a delivery, completing an order, or maintaining equipment.

Following the paragraph, prepare five questions that could be asked to determine if the new employee fully understood your message. Pair up with another student and take turns reading your sets of directions and asking your questions to one another.

After you've completed this exercise, discuss the following:

1. What difficulties did you have as a listener understanding the instructions as given?
2. What steps could you take to make your listening more effective?
3. What might be the consequences of failing to understand these directions exactly?

WRITE INSTRUCTIONS HERE:

WRITE QUESTIONS HERE:

RESPONSE STYLE PRACTICE SHEET

For each of the following three situations, write an example of all five responses.

1. "This co-worker in my carpool is constantly criticizing and complaining about the other people at work. I'm getting sick and tired of these comments. I never hear anything positive about anybody."
Evaluating:

Interpreting:

Supporting:

Questioning:

Paraphrasing:

2. "Wow, I just got fired. My boss walked up to me, gave me my last paycheck and told me that they didn't need me any longer. I didn't even get an explanation why."
Evaluating:

Interpreting:

Supporting:

Questioning:

Paraphrasing:

3. "What do you do when somebody wants to borrow your tools or test equipment? This new assembler doesn't have everything that's needed for the job. I don't mind lending some of my stuff, but I can't keep up with my own work without the tools I need. I hate to be selfish, but I don't know what to do."
Evaluating:

Interpreting:

Supporting:

Questioning:

Paraphrasing:

PARAPHRASING EXERCISE

Paraphrasing—restating the speaker's ideas and feelings in your own words—can be either effective or ineffective depending upon the way it is done. When the response is used sparingly, has a tentative focus, stays only with what is said, does not accuse or evaluate, and captures the full meaning of the speaker's remarks, this response can be a beneficial and necessary tool for the industrial student/worker.

The following list contains several paraphrases; some of them are accurate while others are not. Determine whether the responses are accurate or inaccurate by checking the appropriate box. Compare your answers with the analysis that follows.

Most importantly, remember that even if your paraphrase is off target, it allows the speaker the opportunity to correct any misunderstandings.

1. *Statement*: The supervisor on our crew is a total jerk, always complaining about my work yet never around when I need help.
   Paraphrase: So then, what you're saying is that you think your supervisor isn't treating you fairly by not giving you the help you need?

   _____ Accurate   _____ Inaccurate

2. *Statement*: The motorcycle training program isn't very worthwhile. It was too long, and the information was presented in a drab way. I must say, though, that I did learn something.
   Paraphrase: You learned a lot from that program?

   _____ Accurate   _____ Inaccurate

3. *Statement*: The employees' lounge is a total mess. It's not even comfortable being in there. They might as well close it up.
   Paraphrase: What I hear you saying is that you don't like that room because the furniture is too old.

   _____ Accurate   _____ Inaccurate

4. *Statement*: Wow! Do I have a lot of work ahead of me. But it seems that the more I do, the more new work I'm assigned.
   Paraphrase: You're feeling busy, but you just end up getting more work when you rush?

   _____ Accurate   _____ Inaccurate

5. *Statement*: We never should have pulled out of Vietnam. That was the only reason why we lost that war.
   Paraphrase: So you wanted us to stay in that foreign land, killing and mutilating innocent people while trying to transplant the American dream?

   _____ Accurate   _____ Inaccurate

6. *Statement*: I was kicked out of the house yesterday. I came home, and my bed and clothes were in the front yard. I have nowhere to go from here.

Paraphrase: You're concerned about what you'll do since you've been forced to leave home?

_____ Accurate   _____ Inaccurate

ANALYSIS

1. This statement is on target. It just stays with what has been said.

2. This paraphrase is ineffective because it only picks up on the last idea in the statement, rendering this response incomplete. The first two sentences indicate that this individual did not learn "a lot."

3. This paraphrase is also off because it goes beyond what is said and attempts to offer additional information.

4. This response is effective. It paraphrases the speaker's thoughts *and* feelings.

5. This paraphrase is ineffective because it goes way beyond what was said and has an insulting ring to it. It has twisted the original message to the point of attacking the sender's thoughts. The listener has taken the focus away from the sender by doing this.

6. This paraphrase is effective. It repeats the idea in different words and encourages the speaker to focus on the main problem at hand.

ACTIVE LISTENING: IDENTIFICATION

The following list contains a variety of messages. Following each statement are several responses. Check the one that is most accurately a paraphrase. The best paraphrase is one that restates the feeling and meaning heard. Remember that your goal is to listen only—not to agree or disagree, give advice, or end the feeling.

1. I hate working for this company. They have the cheapest wage and salary program I have ever heard of, and they make us work like dogs.
   ( ) A lot of places are like that. Just forget it.
   ( ) Why do you say that?
   ( ) This company doesn't pay you what you deserve and you're irritated by that?
   ( ) You just complain too much. If it's not one thing it's another.

2. If that supervisor tells me to change the setup on that machine one more time, I'm going to scream!
   ( ) Screaming is not going to solve the problem. You'll probably just end up getting fired.
   ( ) You're furious at being told to change the machine setup so often?
   ( ) What do you mean when you say machine setup?
   ( ) I know what you mean. I worked for a supervisor that did the same thing.

3. Did you see that car? It was a 55 Chevy. I sure hope that I'll be the one who gets to work on that nice ride.
   ( ) Why do you want to work on that car so badly?
   ( ) I hope that I get to work on that car rather than you.
   ( ) You're just looking for some extra work so that you can earn some overtime pay.
   ( ) You're excited about working on that vehicle?

4. Geez, was that customer angry! This is the third time the typewriter has been brought in here, and we still haven't fixed it right. I never know how to handle customers who complain like that.
   ( ) Just be as nice as possible. Remember that the customer always comes first.
   ( ) An angry customer has you wondering how to deal with irate people?
   ( ) What's wrong with that machine?
   ( ) I'd be mad as hell, too, if I brought my typewriter in three times.

5. Did you ever notice that when all the dirty work comes in, I have to do it? That's really unfair.
   ( ) You feel cheated because you have to do all the unpleasant work?
   ( ) You should have seen the work I had to do for my company.
   ( ) What kind of work are you talking about?
   ( ) The Philadelphia 76ers are going to be in town tonight. Do you want to go see the game?

6. That circuits teacher is really a jerk. The other day we were told that we
   would not have any tests for a while; then the teacher comes in and gives
   us a unit exam!

   ( ) Yeah, I had that teacher before, and the same thing happened in our
        class.

   ( ) What was the test on? Do you think you did well?

   ( ) Maybe the teacher had a fight with a student and is taking it out on
        your class.

   ( ) You're irritated with a teacher who gave a test after saying that there
        wouldn't be one?

PARAPHRASING WORK SHEET

From the previous exercises, you have had the chance to identify and write the five response styles. Because we believe strongly in the benefits that come from the paraphrasing response (greater openness, listener attention, and understanding) and because it is not as automatic as the other responses, additional practice will help you perfect this valuable response.

For each of the following situations, identify at least two probable feelings the sender may be experiencing. These feelings may be stated directly or implied. Next, write a paraphrase. Remember, the best paraphrase is one that includes both the speaker's message and feelings.

Example: "The weekends go by so fast, and before you know it, we're back to the grind of another week."

Probable feelings: Anxious, trapped, restless, inhibited, frustrated.

Paraphrase: You feel frustrated when your time off goes by so quickly?

1. "Guess what? I was called for that job interview I've been waiting for. The only problem is that the personnel manager asked me to bring along a résumé, and I've never made one up before."
Possible feelings:

Paraphrase:

2. "My folks have been trying to get me to work in their travel agency after I graduate, but I want to find a job and try to make it on my own."
Possible feelings:

Paraphrase:

3. "I've got three hot reports to get out before Friday, and Lee just called in sick. How am I ever going to get all this work done on time?"
Possible feelings:

Paraphrase:

4. "I'm not sure what's wrong with this generator. We've been doing the regular maintenance on it, but we did have it apart once for cleaning. Now the blasted engine won't even start."
Possible feelings:

Paraphrase:

5. "I really can't stand it any longer. My fiance keeps nagging me to get married. We haven't finished school or saved up enough money. Geez, we don't even have decent jobs yet."
Possible feelings:

Paraphrase:

6. "Jumpin' jelly beans! I can't believe that I did it. That communication skills test I thought I would fail turned out to be easier than I thought. Now I'll be able to get straight A's. Fantastic!"
Possible feelings:

Paraphrase:

7. "Wow! That's the first compliment I ever got from my boss. After my six-month review, my supervisor told me that I'm on the right track for promotion to chief operator.

   Possible feelings:

   Paraphrase:

Chapter 3

SENDING SKILLS

_____ Preview Questions _____

These questions are designed to stimulate your thinking about the chapter information that follows. Answer these questions on the basis of your past and present experiences.

1. What is the difference between skillful and unskillful expression of thoughts and feelings?

2. How would you rate your ability to express your wants, needs, and feelings to others?

3. What specific skills or techniques do you use to express yourself clearly?

4. How do people respond to the opinions you express and the requests you make?

5. In what ways does your ability to express yourself harm or help your job performance?

6. What skills or techniques have you developed for coping with criticism?

7. Describe a conflict situation you are now having or have had in the recent past.

8. What skills or techniques helped you manage the conflict? What would you have liked to have done differently?

——————— Communication Errors: a Dialogue ——————————————————————

Professor Smith approaches the counter as Alexis is working at customer service. The following interaction takes place:

SMITH: Good morning.

ALEXIS: What's so good about it?

SMITH: Well, that no good spouse of mine, Reggie, just up and quit a perfectly good job even though there was no new job to replace it. Well, anyway, Reggie was visiting a sister who's in from California and. . . .

ALEXIS: Look, I have a backlog of orders to fill. What is it that you need?

SMITH: I'm getting to it. Reggie's sister is staying at the city hotel, you know the one that is under investigation for tax evasion and. . . .

ALEXIS: *Please . . . get to the point!*

SMITH: Well . . . I never expected to be treated so poorly. I have to have a replacement for that thing on the back of the car . . . you know, the one that keeps the numbers in place.

ALEXIS: You mean a license plate holder. Why don't you just say that? I swear that some of the customers who come in don't even know the front end from the back end of a car. What else do you need?

SMITH: Are you calling me dumb? I certainly hope not. Anyway, I also need one of those thing-a-ma-jigs that go over the place where you pour in the petrol.

ALEXIS: A gas tank cap. And "petrol?" No one around here uses that word. Where did you come from? Why don't you speak English?

SMITH: If you had traveled as much as I have, you would know that petrol and gasoline mean the same thing. Finally, I have to have one of the lights replaced.

ALEXIS: Which one? There are several lights on a car, you know, or haven't you traveled around the car yet? You've got the interior light, the headlights, the dashboard lights. . . .

SMITH: Well, you don't have to be rude about it. I don't have to stand here and take this abuse. You're the most inconsiderate person I've ever come across. I can just take my business elsewhere!

ALEXIS: Go ahead. Take your business elsewhere. The nearest auto service station is only 200 miles away . . . for a person who travels as much as you do, you should be able to get there and back in less than a day.

Unless you're in the unique position of this auto service dealer who doesn't have to compete with other dealers for business, chances are that being able to communicate effectively and nondefensively with your customers will determine whether or not you will survive as a business.

Certainly, Professor Smith was not effective in communicating the car problems to Alexis. The professor used general language, did not get to the main point right away, filled the message with unimportant detail, and used language that was not understood by the employee.

Yet the professor's communication errors were minor compared to Alexis' who used evaluative rather than descriptive language, expressed feelings ineffectively, put the customer on the defensive, and probably lost future business.

Expressing yourself by using the right language is essential; however, you also need to be aware of how to send messages so that the receiver is more likely to be receptive to listening to them.

This chapter attempts to identify some common problems people have when expressing themselves; it also examines how to send these messages in a nondefensive way, and focuses on how to state feelings, opinions, and requests in conflict situations.

Common Sending Problems

People do not express themselves clearly for many reasons. Some of these problems relate to the message structure while other problems relate to sending the most appropriate message for the situation and relationship.

Four specific problems will be discussed: lack of clarity, defensiveness, lack of assertiveness, and the inability to cope with criticism.

In the first instance, unclear messages often result when we intentionally hide our feelings and experiences from others for fear of rejection. At other times, lack of clarity stems from our inability to put our thoughts and feelings into words. The words we use may not reflect our inner world. Sometimes our words say one thing, and our tone of voice, body posture, and facial expressions say something entirely different, confusing the receivers of our messages.

Sometimes our words say one
thing and our body posture and
attitude say something different,
confusing the receivers of our
messages.

A second problem involves sending messages that create defensive responses. Often we express our thoughts and feelings in ways that make others feel threatened and cause them to react with anger or silence. Defensiveness results when others perceive that we are attacking them, evaluating them, acting superior to them, or are communicating with them for some hidden motive.

A third problem is our inability to communicate "assertively." We often react in two distinct ways when we feel that someone is violating our rights. Many people respond passively by letting others "walk all over" them, saying nothing, sacrificing their needs for the needs of others or for the relationship. Also, we may respond with aggression, which tends to put the other person on the defensive, thereby increasing resentment to a dangerous level in the relationship.

When criticized we often find the
need to justify our behavior.

The final problem we have identified is failing to cope with criticism in a constructive way. When confronted with criticism, we often find the need to justify our behavior in a defensive way rather than to listen for information that may help us improve, correct a serious fault, or deal with manipulative criticism in a tactful way.

All of these problems can be dealt with more effectively if the sender has the appropriate attitudes and skills necessary for communication.

Attitudes and Skills For Effective Expression

Each problem area has corresponding corrective skills that may be employed to bring about more effective communication. Attitudes that reflect a desire to improve relationships underlie each specific skill.

Both the skills and the attitudes for effective expression will be developed fully in individual worksheets throughout this chapter. For now, let's preview the skills necessary to solve these problems.

The problem of lack of clarity can best be countered by separating facts from inferences, carefully reporting our opinions, and using specific language rather than general language. These skills combined with attitudes that reflect openness, honesty, and empathy will improve our communication.

The best deterrent to defensiveness demands the skills of informing statements and tentative expression. Both of these are based on the attitudes of equality, open-mindedness, and honesty.

Effective assertion messages include behavior descriptions, impression checks, feeling messages, consequence statements, request statements, and combinations of these. Assertive skills are based on the assumption that conflict is best managed through a problem solving approach that makes use of direct, honest, and appropriate messages.

Criticism can be handled constructively by analyzing the situation, using fogging, negative assertion, and negative inquiry. Each of these skills reflects basic assumptions about conflict and the judgments of others: conflicts are problems to be solved; individuals are the best judges of their own behavior.

The problems that prevent effective communication (lack of clarity, defensiveness, nonassertion, and difficulty dealing with criticism) may occur in our personal or professional lives. They can be overcome through the development of specific skills and the cultivation of positive, supportive attitudes.

The challenge to you, the communicator, is to incorporate these skills and attitudes into your natural communication system so that you don't seem phony or false but honest, open, and genuine.

CHAPTER 3 CHECK UP

Use these key words from the preceding chapter to complete the following sentences.

defensive	coping with criticism	assertiveness
clarity	passiveness	attitudes
conflicts	aggressiveness	honesty
equality		

1. Communication ＿＿＿＿＿＿ should reveal a desire to improve relationships.

2. Others become ＿＿＿＿＿＿ when you communicate with them in ways that attack or evaluate them.

3. ＿＿＿＿＿＿ is a central attitude that will help you to communicate clearly, nondefensively, and assertively.

4. ＿＿＿＿＿＿ is when we say nothing and let people "walk all over us."

5. It is best when ＿＿＿＿＿＿ to realize that ultimately you are the best judge of your own behavior.

6. Specific versus general language will help you to communicate with ＿＿＿＿＿＿ .

7. Responding to criticism with ＿＿＿＿＿＿ involves lashing out strongly at the critic.

8. ＿＿＿＿＿＿ involves stating your concerns, feelings, impressions, consequences, and intentions.

9. ＿＿＿＿＿＿ are problems to be solved.

10. An attitude that communicates that you are important and valued is one of ＿＿＿＿＿＿ .

_____ Fact Inference Confusion _____

Communication barriers and misunderstandings between people occur for a variety of reasons. One of these reasons involves the failure to separate fact from inference or opinion.

As a result of our different backgrounds, physical traits, and present feelings, we all have formed an infinite number of opinions on topics ranging from politics to the weather. Indeed, the varied opinions we hold are, in part, what make us unique and interesting human beings.

But there is an inherent danger in the opinions we possess, especially if they are strong and/or longstanding. The danger is that subtly, and often unconsciously, we cross the fine line that frequently separates fact from opinion and begin to view our own opinions as factual and, therefore, incapable of being in error.

Let's say, for instance, that you firmly believe women should be given equal opportunity to pursue work in nontraditional occupations such as welding, automotive repair, or electronics. Your friend and co-worker, on the other hand, thinks a woman's place is in the home fulfilling the role of homemaker and mother, or at the very least, doing jobs "nature intended" for women, which include being a teacher, nurse, or secretary.

Now if both of you have forgotten that your opinions are just that— opinions—and subject to change and error, it is highly probable that neither of you will be able to calmly discuss this topic without trying to convince the other of the "facts!"

However, if you both recognize your opinions for what they are— nonfactual—you will be more willing to listen open-mindedly to conflicting views and respect the right of others to think as they do even if you do not personally agree.

Some of the characteristics that separate facts from inferences or opinions are listed next. Statements of fact must be:

1. based on observable sense data (i.e., what you can see, hear, taste, touch, or smell);
2. only about the past or the present, never the future (statements about future events are purely inferential since they have not yet occurred and are, therefore, not observable);
3. objective and devoid of any interpretations, conclusions, or assumptions about what has been observed (i.e., observing a man wearing a multicolored Mohawk haircut *(fact)* and assuming he must like punk rock music *(inference)* goes beyond the observable data).

Statements of inference, in contrast:

1. go beyond what has been observed, as in the case of the "punk rocker" with the Mohawk haircut;
2. are about the past, present, or future;
3. include interpretations, conclusions, or assumptions about what has been observed and are, consequently, subjective.

As a final note, it's often a good idea to state your opinions to others in nonfactual terms by including the use of an "I" message. For example, rather than saying, "Women should have the right to pursue work in nontraditional occupations," say instead, "I have come to believe women should have the right to pursue work in nontraditional occupations." Phrases such as "I think," "To me," "From my point of view," work equally well.

FACT INFERENCE CONFUSION EXERCISE

This exercise will help you to become more aware of the differences between factual and inferential statements and to realize how easy it is to confuse the two.

From the following stories, determine whether the following statements are *factually true* (T), *factually false* (F), or an *inference* of any kind (?).

1. The owner of Webster's Auto Repair was getting ready to close shop for the evening. The owner turned and noticed one of the mechanics stuffing impact and torque wrenches, sockets, and a micrometer into a knapsack. The owner called out to the mechanic, but the mechanic picked up the knapsack, ran out of the garage, hopped into a waiting vehicle, and drove off. The garage owner immediately called the police.

   T F ?   1. The garage owner was named Webster.

   T F ?   2. The mechanic was seen stuffing tools into a knapsack.

   T F ?   3. The man with the knapsack ran out of the garage and into a waiting vehicle.

   T F ?   4. The car with the mechanic in it drove off.

   T F ?   5. The mechanic stole the tools.

2. Terry, who was the first one to punch in on Friday, arrived at Department 325 and noticed that the job which had been worked on Thursday afternoon had been moved to another machinery area. Another casting with *"RUSH"* painted on its side had been moved into Terry's machine. Friday's assignment called for Terry to work on the same machine as on Thursday. The supervisor for Department 325 was at a staff meeting all Friday morning.

   T F ?   1. Terry's work assignment had changed for Friday.

   T F ?   2. The supervisor forgot to tell Terry about a new rush job.

   T F ?   3. Terry was not the first person in Department 325 on Friday morning.

   T F ?   4. The job Terry had been working on had not been moved.

   T F ?   5. Terry has been reassigned to another machinery area.

3. Sandy and Pat, both data processors, are especially good at their jobs. Their combined experience totals some 30 years. They are reliable, hard-working, and very strong individuals. In fact, Sandy lifts weights for a hobby, and Pat plays basketball.

   T F ?   1. This story concerns two men named Sandy and Pat.

   T F ?   2. Sandy and Pat are both hard workers.

   T F ?   3. Sandy is handicapped.

   T F ?   4. Pat and Sandy are married to each other.

   T F ?   5. Sandy never lifted weights.

—————— General Versus Specific Language ————————————————

Perhaps one of the single most frequent causes of misunderstandings between people involves their use of general rather than specific language when communicating. If we become really observant of events around us at home and on the job, chances are we will become aware of these misunderstandings as a daily occurrence: the shipping clerk who mistakenly sends a company its order by air rather than truck because the invoice read *"RUSH"*; the assembly line supervisor who replaces a costly automatic control unit instead of fixing it because the boss said to "get rid of the trouble on the line"; the person who gets upset with a spouse for not helping out with household chores after stating, "You never do anything around this place!" And the list goes on and on.

We tend to be general in our communication with others because we assume they'll know what we mean. The company manager who wrote *"RUSH"* on the order form assumed the shipping clerk would send out the parts that were needed immediately, but not by air, which is twice the cost of truck transport.

The boss assumed the assembly line supervisor would fix rather than replace the automatic control unit after being told, "Get rid of the trouble." The spouse was supposed to have understood that the garbage needed to be taken out when told, "You never do anything around this place!"

It's important to keep in mind that we all have different perceptions of the world around us. No two people will ever process information from their environment in the exact same way. Whenever we receive a message from another person, we interpret that message from our unique point of view, and the meaning we attach to the message may not be the same meaning intended by the sender.

So, to avoid the communication breakdowns caused by language that is general rather than specific, keep in mind the following suggestions:

1. Do not assume that receivers should know what you mean.
2. Avoid the use of general words like "always" and "never." (For example, "You're always late" is *general* while "You were twenty minutes late for work this morning" is *specific*.)
3. Whenever you are expressing needs, wants, thoughts, or feelings state your message in the most concrete or specific words possible. For example, it's better to say, "I need you to answer the phone and take messages while I attend the 1:00 p.m. meeting" rather than "I want you to help out this afternoon."
4. If you question whether the receiver understood your message the way you intended it, encourage the receiver to paraphrase the message. (For example, "I'm not sure I made myself clear. What do you believe I meant by my last comment?")

GENERAL VERSUS SPECIFIC LANGUAGE EXERCISE

Some of the following 15 statements are stated specifically; others are stated generally. Put an "S" next to those statements that are specific—that is, those statements that create a clear picture of what is being said. Put a "G" next to those statements that are general, have broad areas of meaning, and may result in varied interpretations.

_____ 1. Your work station is a mess!

_____ 2. The grass in my back yard needs to be cut today.

_____ 3. That's the third time you've gone jogging this week.

_____ 4. You certainly let your boss take advantage of you.

_____ 5. There's a 30 percent chance of rain in the forecast today.

_____ 6. Send us some of those fancy switches for the control panel.

_____ 7. Place the cost forms for XB4773 on the computer terminal in my office for entry.

_____ 8. Never buy that brand of tool. It is really junk.

_____ 9. From the force of that collision, that car will require extensive repair. It's impossible to fix.

_____ 10. Let's get some help around here. Try pitching in and doing something worthwhile to assist.

_____ 11. The September 13th concert by the Grateful Dead was enjoyable because we had 80 degree sunny weather and third row center seats.

_____ 12. Jan's a poor worker based on that project just turned in.

_____ 13. Lupe has not missed one day's work since beginning this job.

_____ 14. Get the blue '78 Pontiac Firebird in the second row of the used parking lot, section 1.

_____ 15. You're really doing a good job on that project.

Note: Now change the statements that you labeled as "general" to make them more specific and clear.

Absolute Versus Tentative Language

A skill that is closely allied with our effort to be specific rather than general in our communication involves being tentative rather than absolute in the messages we send to others.

We all have our own perception of the objects, events, and people in our environment. We not only perceive these external stimuli through our senses, but we also interpret what these stimuli mean to us and go one step further to formulate opinions about them.

For instance, let's say you look out your living room window and observe a new, expensive Italian sports car parked across the street. You may conclude that the owner must be wealthy. This interpretation may be followed by your personal opinion that money isn't required for happiness or that people should buy American cars as opposed to foreign imports. There's nothing wrong with forming opinions like these; we all do, everyday of our lives. However, we can run into trouble in our relationships with others when we describe our opinions as if they are *always* true or absolute.

Receivers tend to become defensive and unwilling to listen to our opinions with an open mind when these opinions are stated in such strong terms that they leave no room for conflicting views.

Imagine that you work for a company with a strong union and that you personally believe unions are necessary and valuable to protect employee rights. Your friend who works in a nonunionized shop feels just the opposite, and tells you, "Companies, if left alone, would take care of their workers. Unions always cost their members money in dues and don't really provide worker protection." Now, since your views are in direct opposition to your friend's, your response to this statement is likely to be defensive and may trigger an argument.

On the other hand, if your friend had said, "I believe that some companies really care about their workers, like where I work at Acme Tool, and that some unions don't necessarily guarantee worker protection," chances are your reaction to the statement will be different. Why?

Notice the slight change in the wording of the second opinion statement. This time your friend prefaced the opinion with "I believe." This phrase is an example of tentative language as are other such phrases like "I think," "I've come to the conclusion," "It seems to me," "I personally feel," "My belief is," and so on.

Tentative language makes it clear to a receiver that your opinions are just that, *opinions,* not facts and are, therefore, subject to error. Notice, too, that in the second example, your friend omitted the word *always* (an absolute word) and related an opinion to a specific company where an employer provides worker protection.

Elimination of words like "always" and "never" reduces the tendency we all sometimes have to overgeneralize. Avoidance of these words can be especially helpful when we are commenting on another person's behavior.

Examine the difference between saying, "You never listen to me when I talk to you," *(absolute)* versus, "You don't seem interested in listening or talking right now," *(tentative)*. It should be apparent that the first statement stands a greater chance of arousing defensiveness than the latter.

This skill doesn't demand that all of your opinions, however unimportant, be stated tentatively. Chances are it won't make much difference in a conversation if you say, "This is a beautiful day," instead of, "I think this is a beautiful day."

But certainly if you are expressing opinions that are controversial, that may conflict with your receiver's views, or that focus on some aspect of your receiver's behavior, it will probably be more effective to keep your language tentative. By using this skill, you will also be less likely to view your own opinions as "facts" and will, consequently, be more open to conflicting points of view.

ABSOLUTE VERSUS TENTATIVE LANGUAGE EXERCISE

Absolute language reports a definite, unchanging, unqualified point of view, whether or not it is correct. Tentative language, on the other hand, reports what seems to be and acknowledges limitations in our perceptions of things, events, and people—all of which can and do change. Tentative language also opens up the sender to other viewpoints. Put a "T" next to those statements that are stated tentatively and an "A" next to those that are absolute.

_____   **1.** Work breaks should be more than ten minutes long.

_____   **2.** I believe women should have an equal opportunity to compete with men for job openings in the skilled trades.

_____   **3.** Foreign cars are engineered better than American models.

_____   **4.** You need to exercise if you want to stay healthy.

_____   **5.** It appears to me that unemployment contributes to increased crime rates.

_____   **6.** Professor Mendoza is the best teacher in the world.

_____   **7.** The Ricoh 750 is the best copier on the market.

_____   **8.** Getting a student loan is one of several ways of going to school.

_____   **9.** *Computer Age* is the only magazine for people in our field.

_____   **10.** I could be wrong, but I think the Hooters will have a good team this year.

_____   **11.** That gauge isn't accurate. Don't ever trust it.

_____   **12.** Those damn foreign companies with their sweatshops are going to run us out of business.

_____   **13.** It looks to me like the union is our only hope: sometimes I'm not so sure about even that.

_____   **14.** Supervisors spend too much time in meetings and not enough time out on the floor.

_____   **15.** I think Sam made some good points about that grievance you wrote.

Note: Now change all the statements that you labeled "absolute" into "tentative" statements.

######## Informing Versus Ordering Language ########

No one likes to be ordered around: not children, not adults. We put up with orders when we know we must, but resentment often results. Sometimes orders are necessary; we cannot do away with them completely. However, very often we can give information instead of orders. Informing statements will often get the same results without creating defensiveness.

Ordering statements command the receiver of the message to behave in a specific way. They remove any choice or decision making from the receiver. Orders are called "you" messages, and, as such, they direct, control, or command a given course of action.

Whether orders are presented in a polite tone of voice or shouted in an unskillful manner, they usually represent one-way communication which doesn't encourage feedback from the receiver. By giving orders, one sends the message, "I don't want to talk about it. Just do as you are told!"

On the other hand, informing statements provide information that the receiver needs to make a decision. Informing statements reveal thoughts, feelings, wants, and needs. They tell the receiver, "It's important that you know this. I want to share this with you." With adequate information, most receivers will respond in a constructive way. The disclosure of informing statements opens the door for two-way communication and encourages similar sharing from the receiver.

As an example of the difference informing statements can make, let's suppose a manager tells a group of service representatives in the shop, "You've got to write down a customer's complaints more fully on the work order form." Though this "you" message may get the representatives to change their behavior, it may also increase defensiveness and resentment at being told what to do.

Informing messages may be more effective here. To the service representatives, the manager might state, "The technicians spend much of their time figuring out what's wrong with a piece of equipment when specific information is not written on the order form. They'd like to be better informed of the trouble so that they know what to look and listen for."

This response will allow the service representatives the chance to offer their own solutions (e.g., write out the specific complaint on the order form, explain the complaint directly to the technicians, or revise the format of the order form) while not increasing defensiveness or resentment.

Furthermore, the service representatives will, once they've decided on a course of action, be more likely to follow through since they're the ones who proposed the solution.

Again, although orders do have a place in communication, they are not the foundation of a healthy relationship.

INFORMING VERSUS ORDERING LANGUAGE EXERCISE

Some of the following 15 statements give information, while some give orders. Put an "I" in front of the informing statements, and put an "O" in front of the ordering remarks.

_____ **1.** Why don't you close the walk-in cooler door before the compressor overheats?

_____ **2.** I haven't had a date in the last six months.

_____ **3.** A Wednesday night meeting is not convenient for me because I have a dental appointment right after work.

_____ **4.** Let's talk about something other than politics.

_____ **5.** Pizza with pepperoni gives me indigestion.

_____ **6.** Twice you've asked to use my tools, and I said "no." The answer is the same.

_____ **7.** Give me a break! You can't expect me to keep track of everything that happens when the machine breaks down.

_____ **8.** Believe me; you've just got to buy this computer software!

_____ **9.** I need more help to complete these calls this week.

_____ **10.** You have to share the overtime with Ronnie and Kim.

_____ **11.** I feel hurt when you yell at me.

_____ **12.** Shut up! Don't scream when you talk to me.

_____ **13.** My microwave oven needs to be fixed.

_____ **14.** You should go on to a vocational/technical college.

_____ **15.** Don't you know that you have to pick up your boss at 6 o'clock this morning?

Note: Now go back and rewrite each order into an informing statement.

_____ Behavior Descriptions _____

You have probably noticed that the sharing skills we have been discussing are all closely related to one another. This same connection will be seen as we talk about behavior descriptions.

How we interpret other people's behavior influences our thoughts and feelings. If someone's behavior violates our personal rights, prevents us from meeting our needs, or causes us unnecessary inconvenience, we may think we are being treated unfairly and respond with feelings of frustration, irritation, or annoyance.

Expressing feelings is certainly healthy, both physically and psychologically, but such expressions can be even more useful if we let a receiver know what behavior we are reacting to. We cannot force a person to change behavior that is having a negative impact on us, but we can increase the chances of a person changing behavior voluntarily when we describe that behavior in specific, factual, nonjudgmental terms.

Notice the difference between saying to someone, "You've really been inconsiderate lately," compared to, "You've borrowed my reference manuals twice this week without asking me if I needed to use them."

In the first instance, your receiver may not only become defensive at being called inconsiderate but also may have no idea what behavior led you to make that judgment. In the second instance, the receiver now knows precisely what behavior you are reacting to, minus the personal judgment you make about the behavior.

The receiver is more likely to ask permission to borrow your tools next time (which is really what you wanted all along) because you've clearly identified the behavior, and you've avoided any evaluation of character, motives, or intentions, thereby reducing defensiveness.

We can never know for certain what motivates people to behave as they do, so it's wise to simply describe the behavior we observe with our senses and then identify how we are feeling in response to that behavior.

Behavior descriptions should meet the following criteria:

1. They should report only behaviors we can observe with our senses.
2. They should exclude any evaluation of the behavior or statement of what we believe may be the feelings, motives, or intentions that prompted the behavior.
3. They should be specific and tentative rather than general and absolute (i.e., avoid words like "always" and "never").

As a final note, you may find it helpful to describe others' behaviors that affect you positively and not just negatively as we've been discussing thus far.

For example, let's say your friend makes the following statement to you: "When you cancelled your plans to go North last weekend so you could help me move, I was really grateful because I couldn't have done it alone." This comment shares a very specific behavior, along with personal feelings and results of the behavior. You would probably feel more appreciated for your actions if your friend makes this kind of statement rather than just saying, "Thanks for helping me move."

Describing behaviors of others that affect us positively not only reinforces such behaviors but promotes relationships in which feelings of warmth, caring, and appreciation are fostered.

BEHAVIOR DESCRIPTIONS EXERCISE

Some of the following statements describe *only* observable behavior while others deal with motives, feelings, attitudes, etc. Put an "X" next to those statements that describe specific behaviors *only*.

_____ **1.** Robin, when you took the reservations for Jones' trip to Puerto Escondido, you made a funny face.

_____ **2.** You just turned and walked away from me when I lit up my cigar.

_____ **3.** Chris, you gave me a dirty look for telling an ethnic joke at the party.

_____ **4.** You straightened your tie, buttoned your suit coat, brushed back your hair, and then entered the room.

_____ **5.** Kelly, you were really excited when you got that new job offer.

_____ **6.** I just saw you punch in on Stewart's time card.

_____ **7.** You were really annoyed when I wouldn't change vacations with you.

_____ **8.** Sandy, you answered the phone, called the service department, and said Job #2217 was ready.

_____ **9.** Shawn, apparently you don't have time to play softball with us this year.

_____ **10.** Alex, you weren't at the concert; you didn't make the party; and you didn't go to the game either.

_____ **11.** Stacey, you were rude to that customer because you're prejudiced.

_____ **12.** You didn't check these parts for the correct size.

_____ **13.** By the way you twisted the ends of your hair, I could tell you were preoccupied.

_____ **14.** From the slight droop of your lips and mouth, I could tell you were sad about what the boss said.

_____ **15.** Because you punched in late this morning, I had to work alone.

Note: Change all non-behavior description statements into statements that describe observable behavior only.

WRITING BEHAVIOR DESCRIPTIONS WORK SHEET

Use specific, clear language to write six behavior descriptions. These should present behaviors that please you in three situations and behaviors that upset you in the other three incidents.

1.

2.

3.

4.

5.

6.

——————— Constructive Feeling Messages ————————————————————

As human beings, we all experience a wide range of emotions. Psychologists theorize that those individuals who skillfully express emotions to others tend to experience a higher degree of physical and psychological health, which is often the result of more satisfying interpersonal relationships, than those individuals who do not.

We could all lessen misunderstandings, reduce stress, and avoid unnecessary conflict if we learned to voice our feelings constructively at home and in the workplace. The skill of expressing feelings doesn't imply sharing our deepest inner emotions with everyone and anyone. The inappropriate expression of feelings can be just as destructive as the failure to express any feelings at all. However, more people seem to fall into the category of underexpressing rather than overexpressing their feelings; therefore, our goal is to achieve a balance between these two extremes.

Four general guidelines can help us determine when expressing our feelings is appropriate. Feelings should be expressed

1. in ongoing relationships (e.g., parent-child, husband-wife, friend-friend, etc.);
2. when there is a greater likelihood of helping the relationship rather than harming it;
3. in the face of conflict that threatens the relationship;
4. when the expression of those feelings moves gradually to a deeper level of sharing (i.e., you don't share highly personal feelings with someone you've just met).

Knowing when to express feelings is not enough. Equally important is knowing how to express them. Constructive feeling messages contain these elements:

1. an "I" message which makes it clear to a receiver that you are claiming ownership and accepting responsibility for the feelings you are expressing;
2. identification of the precise feeling you are experiencing (e.g., hurt, annoyance, happiness, uncertainty, confidence, etc);
3. a description of the behavior of the person you are responding to emotionally.

The following are examples of how these elements can be combined into effective expressions of feelings:

1. "When you use my car and then don't refill the gas tank, I feel irritated."
2. "I'm so pleased with the seven extra hours you've put in on the blueprints."
3. "When you tried to talk to me during the meeting, I got really upset because I missed the change in work hours the supervisor was explaining."

In the beginning, you may feel awkward and mechanical using this skill, but with practice, feeling messages will become a part of your overall style of communication and become a natural way of responding to the people with whom you interact.

CONSTRUCTIVE FEELING MESSAGES EXERCISE

Following are 15 statements, some of which describe feelings directly and specifically. Put an "X" next to those statements that constructively describe what the speaker is feeling.

_____ 1. I feel it's time for us to take a break.

_____ 2. I'm really grateful you loaned me your car while mine was being repaired.

_____ 3. I get annoyed when you turn up the stereo while I'm studying.

_____ 4. My feelings are hurt when you tell me I'm inconsiderate of others.

_____ 5. You are such an easygoing person.

_____ 6. This darn fighting all the time is a pain. It has me really worried.

_____ 7. Apart from all the work I have to do, I feel a sense of accomplishment with this job.

_____ 8. I'm surprised that you could say that to the supervisor. I thought you did it just right, though.

_____ 9. I don't feel good about being here; Sam's always complaining about something.

_____ 10. I feel that going on the second shift if you don't have to is really stupid.

_____ 11. I feel you could practice more.

_____ 12. When you're late from work, I feel concerned.

_____ 13. I feel nervous about that speech assignment coming up.

_____ 14. I am clumsy—always have been, always will be.

_____ 15. I feel like I'm on top of the world.

Note: Now go back and rewrite those statements that unskillfully express feelings so that they clearly state the speaker's feelings.

WRITING CONSTRUCTIVE FEELING MESSAGES WORK SHEET

Refer to the work sheet titled "Writing Behavior Descriptions" on page 61. For each of the behavior description statements you wrote, add an appropriate feeling message. Use the form, "When you. . . . , I feel. . . ."

1. When you _____

_____ I feel _____ .

2. When you _____

_____ I feel _____ .

3. When you _____

_____ I feel _____ .

4. When you _____

_____ I feel _____ .

5. When you _____

_____ I feel _____ .

6. When you _____

_____ I feel _____ .

_____ Consequence Statements _____

All of our actions have consequences; these consequences affect our lives in many ways, both positively and negatively. This simple fact of life comes home to us in countless ways. Our job performance, when reviewed, can be the source of reward or punishment. Our conduct on the job can either favorably impress or turn off co-workers. Our behavior in public places can win the respect of family and friends, or it can get us arrested. What we do can have a very definite impact on others and our relationship with them.

The consequences of our actions can be tangible and concrete, or they may be intangible. Thomas Gordon, Robert Bolton, and other communication experts have written about the importance of tangible and concrete effect statements when expressing feelings to others. They note the strengths of telling others how their behavior has real, lasting effects on our time, money, work, possessions, and effectiveness on the job. These tangible, concrete effects can be measured in terms of gains, savings, or losses. As such, they represent the most potent form of consequence by showing how someone's behavior affects us directly.

Different from the tangible, but in many ways no less important, are the intangible effects that occur when others take action that has a definite impact on our lives as well. The feelings we enjoy or suffer through, the sense of accomplishment or being cared for, and the notion of power or belonging can directly or indirectly spring from our reaction to the behavior of others. Hearing that someone loves you, that your son wants a Mohawk haircut, or that a good friend is moving away produce effects which cannot be measured by a clock, in your pocketbook, or in your productivity, yet the consequences affect you in very significant ways.

Both tangible and intangible effects may be positive or negative. They can save, enhance, add to, or enrich; on the other hand, they similarly can cost, diminish, waste, or destroy. Effective communication requires the sharing of consequences both positive and negative, tangible and intangible. Consequence statements provide information that clarifies our feeling reactions and makes our messages more appropriate to the receiver.

Consequence statements answer the question "why?" They provide a "because" for thoughts and feelings. Here are some examples of these statements:

"... because that costs me money that I don't have."
"... because I have to spend extra time repairing the equipment."
"... because I only had time to type three letters today."

These, of course, are tangible, negative effects; they could also be positive:

"... because I save money and time when you rebuild that carburetor for me."
"... because I saved extra work and trips when you helped me move across town last week."

Likewise, the intangibles can be stated either positively or negatively:

"... because I feel really happy."
"... because I think I really belong to this group."
"... because it damages my reputation with the rest of the employees."
"... because I can't cope with things."

In short, consequence statements inform others of the effects their behavior is having on us. These statements need to be honest, nonthreatening expressions of our perceived reactions to their behaviors.

CONSEQUENCE STATEMENTS EXERCISE

Label the following statements as "T" for tangible, or "I" for intangible.

_____ 1. . . . because I have to spend money on a new television set.

_____ 2. . . . because my feelings are hurt.

_____ 3. . . . because my calculator doesn't work anymore, and I need it.

_____ 4. . . . because I was unable to complete the work on time.

_____ 5. . . . because I could be injured if we have an accident.

_____ 6. . . . because I have to spend three hours redoing the work.

_____ 7. . . . because I can't go as fast as you do.

_____ 8. . . . because I'm late for work and get docked for pay.

_____ 9. . . . because I'm embarrassed to say I don't know.

_____ 10. . . . because I get annoyed and aggravated.

_____ 11. . . . because that makes me look bad.

_____ 12. . . . because then people won't believe me.

_____ 13. . . . because I think you don't like me.

_____ 14. . . . because my standing in the community is lessened.

_____ 15. . . . because I lose my place and have to start over.

WRITING CONSEQUENCE STATEMENTS WORK SHEET

Provide consequence statements for the following messages:

1. When you called me a fool in front of the class, I felt hurt because

2. When you smoke cigarettes, I feel concerned because

3. When you said I didn't need a whole new stereo system, I was relieved because

4. When you start talking to me as you are walking into another room, I get upset because

5. When you talk to me when I'm on the phone with a customer, I feel frustrated because

6. When you leave your clothes all over the living room, I get irritated because

7. When you borrow my car and return it to me empty of gas with empty beer cans and pizza boxes in the back, and scratches in the paint on the hood, I'm furious because

8. When you change my work assignment five minutes before I'm supposed to start, I get confused because

9. When you poured the antifreeze in the oil fill spout, I was annoyed because

10. When you smoke cigarettes in our enclosed work area, I feel violated because

THREE PART CONSTRUCTIVE FEELING MESSAGES WORK SHEET

Following are six situations in which feelings are not effectively described by the speaker. Write a clear, direct message that includes a behavior description, identifies a feeling, and states a consequence.

1. Leslie, an employee at a local welding company, had completed the day's work and was about to punch out when the supervisor came over to compliment Leslie on the job that had been completed that day. The supervisor said, "Nice work, Leslie. We couldn't have done it without you." What could the supervisor have said to Leslie to more clearly express appreciation?

   When you _____

   _____ I feel _____ because I _____

   _____ .

2. Your roommates continually leave clothes lying around, don't wash the dishes, and say they are too busy to help you scrub and vacuum the apartment. You yell at them saying, "You never do anything around this place. I wish you had moved in with someone as sloppy as you." What could you say to express your feelings more effectively?

   When you _____

   _____ I feel _____ because I _____

   _____ .

3. When Lupe thought there was real favoritism being shown on the job assignments, Lupe blew up at Jesse and said, "Sure you're happy with your jobs; you're the boss's pet. You've been playing up to the boss since you were first hired." How could Lupe better express these feelings?

   When you _____

   _____ I feel _____ because I _____

   _____ .

4. Robin was very grateful for Terry's help when they were planning the group itinerary for a trip to Tahiti. Robin wasn't sure how to share this gratitude and simply said, "Thanks." What could Robin have said to express these feelings more clearly?

   When you _____

   _____ I feel _____ because I _____

   _____ .

5. Lou and Jo were having lunch in the cafeteria and discussing politics. Their discussion became somewhat intense, and Jo interrupted Lou several times before Lou could finish making a point. Finally, Lou said to Jo, "Quit interrupting me! Can't you give me a chance to say what I think before you butt in?" What could Lou have said to express these feelings more effectively to Jo?

When you _____

_____ I feel _____ because I _____

_____ .

6. Now that Jan is out of school and working full time as a data processing technician, Jan's parents have been making suggestions and subtle hints to Jan about how to budget money. Jan is capable of managing finances and has responded to these suggestions by stating, "Why are you always telling me how I should spend my money? I'm old enough to do what I want with it!" What could Jan have said to express these feelings more clearly?

When you _____

_____ I feel _____ because I _____

_____ .

———— Impression Checks ————————————————————————

Impression checks are responses to someone's verbal or nonverbal communication which share an impression of that person's message in an open-minded, nonevaluative way and which invite a response from the person.

As a communication tool, impression checks help the sender to verify assumptions or inferences that are made in response to another's words or actions. Impression checks provide a way to confirm what you're thinking about other people without always having to ask a question.

Clear impression checks should do four things:

1. State your impression or inference of another person; that is, what you think that individual is wanting, needing, thinking, feeling, or going to do. For example, "I get the impression you want some time to yourself."

2. Present your impression in an open-minded or tentative way which suggests "I may be wrong," by using phrases such as, "It seems" or "It looks as if. . . ."

3. Express your impressions in a nonevaluative manner. The tone of your voice should not imply that you're judging, belittling, or putting down the sender. "It looks like you really botched the computer program this time," makes an evaluation of the sender and should be avoided.

4. Invite a response by using either a rising inflection at the end of your statement or by a very short question. Questions such as "Are you? Am I right? Is that it?" invite a response without taking attention away from the impression check. These very brief questions seek to verify the accuracy of the impression. Avoid a longer, more involved question that will open a whole new area of concern.

Now that you know what impression checks are, let's discuss when you might use these tools.

Let's suppose someone has said or done something that you don't completely understand. You have some idea of what the sender is feeling, wanting, needing, or thinking, but you're not sure. At this point you may ask a question, or you may just pretend you know what's going on and not say anything. Sometimes a question will clarify meanings; other times you'll only get a vague response.

Impression checks give you another tool in your communication skills toolbox to use at times like this. They help to start conversations when you want to show some empathy for the other person or when you need clarification of some inference you have made. Impression checks have to be used with a curious, questioning tone of voice that communicates your interest and concern.

Impression checks encourage the other person to confirm your inferences or to show you where they are incorrect. Either way, this skill enables you to show that you are listening and care enough to try to understand the other person.

IMPRESSION CHECKS EXERCISE

Some of the following statements effectively state an individual's impressions, while others do not. Place an "X" next to those statements that effectively state impressions.

——————— 1. Fran, it sure looks like you woke up on the wrong side of the bed.

——————— 2. By your hesitation to say yes, I get the idea that Wednesday will not be a good day for us to meet. Right?

——————— 3. You're late again. What the hell's the matter with you?

——————— 4. Why are you always so rude?

——————— 5. I might be wrong, but I get the impression that you feel disappointed because you just flunked the test?

——————— 6. You seem disappointed to me. What did I do wrong?

——————— 7. I get the idea that you made another silly mistake.

——————— 8. What's got you so excited? You're not always this excited.

——————— 9. Shelby, I get the idea that you think I'm having trouble with this work, right?

——————— 10. Looks to me like you're thinking of quitting here and starting at Acme Engineering?

——————— 11. It seems to me that you should find an apartment closer to your job. Don't you agree?

——————— 12. I get the feeling you're looking forward to your vacation out west, right?

——————— 13. My impression is that you don't agree with the union's demand for a four-day work week. Is this true?

——————— 14. I'm getting the idea that you're happy about Dale's promotion. Am I right?

——————— 15. It appears to me that you are being too hasty.

Note: Rewrite those statements that you did not "X" so that they become effective impression checks.

WRITING IMPRESSION CHECKS WORK SHEET

Refer to the work sheet titled "Writing Behavior Descriptions" on page 61. For each of the behavior descriptions, write an appropriate impression checking statement.

1. When you _____

_____ it seems to me that _____

_____ .

2. When you _____

_____ I get the impression _____

_____ .

3. When you _____

_____ I sense that _____

_____ .

4. When you _____

_____ it looks like _____

_____ .

5. When you _____

_____ I thought that _____

_____ .

6. When you _____

_____ it appears as if _____

_____ .

_____ Request Statements _____

Being able to communicate through the use of behavior descriptions, impression checks, feeling messages, and consequence statements is necessary if others are to understand you better and react to you more positively. Combining behavior descriptions, feeling messages, and consequence statements will often get people to modify their actions in a way that reduces the concern at hand.

For example, you tell a friend, "I feel irritated when you leave your clothes lying around the living room in our apartment because I have to spend my time and energy to put your clothes back where they belong."

This may be the first time that your roommate has come to know that such behavior is affecting you negatively. Your roommate may respond with, "Oh, I'm sorry; I didn't know that bothered you. You never said anything before, so I thought it was okay. Now that I know it irritates you, I'll make sure I put my clothes in my own room."

Getting people to modify their behavior is the goal, and if others change without having to be directly asked that is great. However, sometimes people don't realize that their behavior is having a negative effect on you, even when you tell them, or they do not know how to relieve the irritation that you're experiencing. In such situations, *request statements* are the next logical messages you will want to send. Requests are polite statements that directly and specifically ask someone to change a behavior in a way that gets your needs met and that maintains the quality of the relationship.

Requests may seek the permission of others for actions you want to perform, "I would like to have off on Saturday the 18th"; or they may ask for help from others, "Can you help me understand this diagram in the service manual?"; or they may ask for cooperation from others, "Let's work together toward a solution of the work schedule, one which meets both of our needs."

The essential parts of a request statement are as follows:

1. Requests should be direct. You must state directly what you need, want, or would like to see happen.
2. Requests must be specific. You need to tell others exactly what you are asking them to do.
3. Requests must allow for a freedom of response. Be open-minded and realize that people may say "no" to your request because they are unable or unwilling to do what you ask. Listen to alternative suggestions from others that may meet both your needs as effectively as your original request.

Request statements are most helpful for interpersonal relationships when they directly ask the other, specifically express your needs, openly accept alternative suggestions, and actively encourage a freedom of response.

REQUESTS VERSUS NON-REQUESTS EXERCISE

Place an "R" next to the following statements that make direct and specific requests. Those statements that are not specific and direct requests should be left blank.

_____ 1. Please hand me that 7/16-inch socket.

_____ 2. Do I get angry when you come in late on Monday mornings?

_____ 3. We should change the channel so we can see the movie called *Don't Look Now.*

_____ 4. The RGB electric typewriter needs to have a semiannual cleaning.

_____ 5. I want you to go to Quality Plating to pick up the reconditioned parts that I have on order.

_____ 6. Since I've been putting in overtime at work, could you help me get supper on the table?

_____ 7. Employee to boss: "You know, it's been almost a year and a half since I had my last raise."

_____ 8. I want you to pick me up for work tomorrow because my car won't be repaired until Wednesday.

_____ 9. I want to talk to you about the low rating you gave me on my work evaluation last month.

_____ 10. Wouldn't it be a good idea to move on to the next item on the agenda? This meeting is running too long already.

_____ 11. I'd like you to let me know before you use that new numerical control machine so that I can see how it works.

_____ 12. What do you know about the settings on this new copier?

_____ 13. Can you help me file this batch of office equipment requests that came in this morning?

_____ 14. Would it be possible for you to change vacation days with me next week?

_____ 15. Why can't I have the same assignments as everybody else? I can do everything they can.

Note: Now change the non-requests into requests.

CONFLICT SITUATIONS—ROLE PLAY WORK SHEET

Following are three conflict situations. There is space at the bottom for you to describe a conflict you've had or are having. For each situation, you are asked to be open-minded and explain both sides of the conflict. Then construct several messages that show your assertive options in these situations. Following is an example.

> *EXAMPLE:* The person who relieves you at work has demanding family responsibilities and is constantly coming in late. This person is your friend, so you don't want to tell the boss. Three times, however, you've missed some important engagements because you left work too late. You've mentioned something before in passing, but this person keeps showing up late, including today.

> **Your Viewpoint:**   I need to be off work on time. I need to meet other important obligations.

> **Other Viewpoint:** My friend is having difficulty coming to work on time because of family responsibilities.

ASSERTIVE OPTIONS

Behavior Description: You came to work 25 minutes late today, and this is the third time in the past two weeks.

Feeling Message: I feel upset that I have to stay late but also trapped because I think I can't do anything about it.

Consequence Statement: I have to miss some important engagements and spend my free time at work when I'd rather be somewhere else.

Impression Check: I get the impression that your family responsibilities are making you late. Are they?

Request Statement: I would like to know how much longer this is going to continue and if there is some way I can be notified earlier when you can't come to work on time.

YOUR COMBINED ASSERTIVE STATEMENT

When you came to work 25 minutes late today, and this is the third time in the past two weeks, I get the impression that your family responsibilities are making you late? I would like to know if there is some way I can be notified earlier when you can't be to work on time.

OR

When you came to work 25 minutes late today, and this is the third time in the past two weeks, I feel upset and also trapped because I have had to miss some important engagements.

1. Ardon Caterers inform you that they will cater your wedding for $200.00, plus food. You provide most of the food, and Ardon gives you a bill for $1,000.00, which you feel is totally unreasonable. You pay only $500.00. Ardon calls to demand the rest of the money.

Your Viewpoint:

Ardon's Viewpoint:

ASSERTIVE OPTIONS

Behavior Description:

Feeling Message:

Consequence Statement:

Impression Check:

Request Statement:

YOUR COMBINED ASSERTIVE STATEMENT

2. You're concerned about a co-worker at the company where you're both employed. You've become very good friends, but you notice that your friend has come to work intoxicated several times in the last few weeks since being denied a recent promotion. When you asked about this behavior, your friend yelled at you and told you to mind your own business. You believe this person needs your friendship more than ever.

Your Viewpoint:

Your Friend's Viewpoint:

ASSERTIVE OPTIONS

Behavior Description:

Feeling Message:

Consequence Statement:

Impression Check:

Request Statement:

YOUR COMBINED ASSERTIVE STATEMENT

3. Your employer had told you that your vacation request was approved. Two days before the vacation is to begin, you have heard through the grapevine that your vacation request is to be denied. You've already made extensive plans to travel and will lose money if you have to cancel. Your supervisor is now telling you about the denial of your time off.

Your Viewpoint:

Supervisor's Viewpoint:

ASSERTIVE OPTIONS

Behavior Description:

Feeling Message:

Consequence Statement:

Impression Check:

Request Statement:

YOUR COMBINED ASSERTIVE STATEMENT

4. Your Conflict:

Your Viewpoint:

The Other Viewpoint:

                                                  ASSERTIVE OPTIONS

Behavior Description:

Feeling Message:

Consequence Statement:

Impression Check:

Request Statement:

                              YOUR COMBINED ASSERTIVE STATEMENT

——— Coping With Criticism ————————————————————

Communication, to be effective, must be conducted in an atmosphere where the participants feel "valued." Certainly, communicating with others who are critical, manipulative, inattentive, and closed-minded is frustrating and unproductive. Of course, some constructive criticism is necessary if we are to become aware of our shortcomings and find new and more effective ways of behaving.

Dealing with criticism and responding nondefensively may be one of the most difficult and challenging aspects of effective communication. The natural tendency to become defensive when we are criticized may result in a negative, upward spiral of defensiveness, which may provoke insults, put-downs, and hurt feelings.

Manuel Smith, in his book *When I Say No, I Feel Guilty*, suggests three specific communication techniques an employee can use to cope effectively with criticism.[1] These three skills are "fogging," "negative assertion," and "negative inquiry."

Fogging

Fogging is a technique of calmly acknowledging unfair criticism without agreeing or disagreeing with it. The fogger is then allowed to make a judgment of what to do with the criticism: believe it, challenge it, or discard it. Fogging is based on the assumption that the individual is the ultimate judge of criticized behavior.

For example, to the boss who says, "Fran, your uniform is a mess, and you look like a slob," Fran might respond by saying, "Perhaps my uniform is too messy, maybe I do look like a slob." This fogging response shows that Fran was listening and acknowledged the criticism without being defensive or without agreeing. Fran's indifferent, matter-of-fact tone of voice communicates the unspoken part of fogging: "I'll decide." Fogging, then, is a way of acknowledging the criticism without "buying" into it.

Negative Assertion

Negative assertion is a technique where you agree with valid criticism without having to apologize or give excuses. This has the dual effect of allowing you to acknowledge your shortcomings and to reduce your critic's negative feelings. Negative assertion is based on the assumption that to "err is human," and the best way to deal with our mistakes is to strongly agree with the criticism.

For example, after you offered to pick Jan up from work, you completely forgot until an hour later. When you finally arrived, Jan said, "You forgot to pick me up. I nearly froze my toes off waiting for you." Rather than giving excuses, it might be best to say, "Geez, I did forget to pick you up. I'm sorry. That's the dumbest thing I've done all week." This response strongly agrees with the criticism without offering excuses, placing blame, or becoming defensive. Negative assertion helps us accept our mistakes and learn from them.

Negative Inquiry

Negative inquiry is a technique requiring the active questioning of the critic for more specifics or for more criticism. The desired effect is that the criticism, if valid, will help you to improve, and if unfair, will exhaust your critic's concerns

[1]Manuel Smith, When I Say No, I Feel Guilty (New York: Bantam Books, 1975) pp. 100–123.

and thereby reduce defensiveness. The assumption behind negative inquiry is that through active questioning, you can determine if the criticism is valid or unfair. Your concerned, curious tone of voice should say, "I'm confused; I need more information." Questions such as, "What is it about my. .? How does my . . . affect . . .? What specifically did I . . .? What else am I not doing effectively?" help the critic to explain in greater detail the nature of the criticism and to disclose any unmet needs to you.

For example, the crew leader has just told you that your work is not up to company standards. You're confused and say, "What is it about my performance that is less than standard? . . . Is there anything else that I'm not doing well on the job?" These kinds of questions will generate more open communication between you and your critic and will help you to decide whether the criticism is valid or unfair and whether you need to respond further with fogging or negative assertion.

Use the exercise which follows on "coping skills" to practice these three techniques for dealing with criticism.

COPING SKILLS WORK SHEET

Write an example of each of the three coping skills for the nine statements of criticism listed below.

1. We give you people a uniform allowance, and you come to work looking like slobs. What do you do, spend it all on booze or dope? You're a disgrace to this company.

Fogging

Negative Assertion

Negative Inquiry

2. If you'd pay closer attention to me, I wouldn't have these hassles with inspection. I distinctly told you only one anchor hole goes in the JS708. The JA710 gets two anchor holes. Pay attention!

Fogging

Negative Assertion

Negative Inquiry

3. If you keep bouncing those tanks around, we'll all get blown up. You don't have to be so damn careless around others. But then you don't care! You know it all.

Fogging

Negative Assertion

Negative Inquiry

4. Quality control just returned three more housings for rework. The machinery tolerances aren't close enough. You did all three jobs. What have you got to say this time?
Fogging

Negative Assertion

Negative Inquiry

5. You've been taking breaks that are too long this past week. We give each employee ten minutes for break, and you were gone at least 15 minutes yesterday, Tuesday, and today. What's the story here anyway?
Fogging

Negative Assertion

Negative Inquiry

6. Every time there's a rejection of your work, you blame it on the prints. It's always engineering's fault! Sometimes I wonder if you even know how to read those prints.
Fogging

Negative Assertion

Negative Inquiry

7. How come you always get the best machines to work on? You never get stuck with the relics that I have to use. How did you get such pull with the boss anyway?
Fogging

Negative Assertion

Negative Inquiry

8. Your work is overrated. I don't think you're working at labor grade #7. The flaws in those last two orders are proof enough for me. You might think you're doing a great job, but you're just fooling yourself.
Fogging

Negative Assertion

Negative Inquiry

9. Maybe I deserve that bad evaluation; maybe I'm not perfect yet. But, what help have you been? You criticize without offering any help at all. You complain about my work but don't take time to show me how to improve. You're responsible, too! Don't just blame me!

Fogging

Negative Assertion

Negative Inquiry

Demonstration Talk

Effective sending skills are especially important in public speaking situations. Public speaking provides an individual with the opportunity to inform or persuade an audience and, as such, is a valuable communication activity. Public speaking allows you to apply the skills of effective interpersonal communication. In fact, the skills that you use when communicating on a one-to-one basis can also be used to communicate successfully to 10 or 10,000. You need to know your listeners, have good eye-contact, speak clearly, use specific language, etc.

Research suggests that your public speaking ability may determine your success in school and on the job. When Kathleen Kendall surveyed some 478 adults in New York state, she asked, "Do real people ever give speeches?" The results indicated that 55-63 percent of these adults gave at least one speech in the last two years to an audience of ten or more people.[2] These speeches were frequently job related and of an informative nature. Further, she found that as your education and income level increase, so do the number of speeches you may be asked to give. While speaking opportunities increase with job responsibilities, Kendall implies that successful public speaking is the key that opens doors to advancement on the job.

The following demonstration talk assignment will provide you with an opportunity to practice the skills of effective public speaking by teaching your audience how to do something, how to make something, or how something works.

[2]Kathleen Kendall, "Do Real People Ever Give Speeches?" *SPECTRA*, (Annandale, VA: Speech Communication Association December, 1985) p. 2.

DEMONSTRATION TALK ASSIGNMENT

ASSIGNMENT

Prepare and present an original set of instructions for performing a simple task so that members of the audience will be able to follow the instructions exactly as you've explained.

QUALIFICATIONS

A. Time limit—four to seven minutes.

B. Use at least two authoritative sources, such as magazines, books, reference material, or expert opinions. Acknowledge these sources either within the context of the speech or at the end of the speech.

C. Use at least one visual aid during your talk. Blackboards, graphs, charts, models, diagrams, and/or the actual object are all suitable visual aids.

D. Include two types of verbal supports to reinforce your ideas. These may include:

    1. Examples—either real or hypothetical

    2. Testimony—the actual words (quotation) of authoritative sources or a paraphrase of the gist of their words.

    3. Statistics—numbers showing relationships or trends.

    4. Comparison—showing similarities between objects from the same class (literal comparison) or objects from different classes (figurative comparison).

    5. Illustration—an expanded example in detailed story form, either factual or hypothetical (imaginary but believable).

    6. Explanation—a verbal description of the process, a definition of terms, or an analysis of component parts.

    7. Demonstration—using visual aids to show, demonstrate, or clarify.

E. Complete the following six-step procedure.

    1. Choose a topic that explains "How to do something" (rebuild a ratchet), "How to make something" (a stereo speaker system), or "How something works" (automobile ignition system). The topic should be one you're interested in and one that offers new and important ideas to the audience.

    2. Research your topic by getting additional materials from the library, interviewing workers in the field, or reviewing notes/books from classes you've taken in the past.

    3. Organize your speech into an introduction, body, and conclusion. Use the outline method which follows next.

    4. Study your outline. Make sure examples and main ideas are clear, and make sure you can explain them.

    5. Practice in as realistic a way as possible. Use visual aids as you practice; ask others to listen and provide feedback; and practice before a mirror and into a tape recorder.

6. Delivery should be as natural as possible with good body posture and a clear voice. Use extended eye contact, looking at one or two people at a time for four to eight seconds, then randomly moving on to the next person.

SPEECH OUTLINE

I. Introduction
   A. Attention-getting opening remarks—capture the audience's attention by relating an experience, asking a thought-provoking question, or making a startling statement.
   B. Clear statement of purpose—tell the audience specifically what your speech is about and why the audience should listen.
   C. Preview of steps in procedure—briefly highlight the major points to be covered.
II. Body
   A. First step
      1. Use of verbal supports to clarify ideas
   B. Second step
      1. Verbal supports
   C. Third step
      1. Verbal supports
III. Conclusion
   A. Review steps in procedure—briefly summarize the major points covered
   B. Restate purpose—what the speech was about and how audience will benefit
   C. Appropriate closing remarks—may include precautions, recommendations, or suggestions for successfully following the instructions

OUTLINE FORM

I. Introduction

    A. Attention-getting opening remark

    B. Clear statement of purpose

    C. Preview of steps

       1.

       2.

       3.

II. Body

    A. First step

       1. Support:

    B. Second step

       1. Support:

    C. Third step

       1. Support:

III. Conclusion

A. Review of steps

B. Restatement of purpose

C. Closing remarks

CRITIQUE SHEET—DEMONSTRATION TALK

3 points = Good
2 points = Average
1 point = Poor

A. The Verbal Message

_____ **1.** Begins by getting the audience's attention

_____ **2.** States clearly the speech topic/purpose

_____ **3.** Previews the body of the speech

_____ **4.** Speech topic is unique and relevant

_____ **5.** Ideas followed a logical sequence

_____ **6.** Smooth transitions from point to point

_____ **7.** Conclusion reviewed the main ideas

_____ **8.** Finished with appropriate closing remark

_____ **9.** Shares two authoritative sources

_____ **10.** Speech conformed to time limit; was delivered on assigned day

B. The Nonverbal Message

_____ **1.** Maintained eye contact with the audience

_____ **2.** Speaker was fluent and conversational; effective volume and vocal variety

_____ **3.** Free, easy natural gestures

_____ **4.** Visual aid handled well

_____ **5.** Avoids "um's," "er's," "ah's," etc.

C. Overall Effectiveness

_____ **1.** Speaker was poised and enthusiastic

_____ **2.** Material seemed accurate, honest, free of propaganda

_____ **3.** Speaker accomplished purpose: demonstrated how to do something, how to make something, how something works

_____ TOTAL SCORE

Chapter 4

WRITING SKILLS

1. Identify the types of writing you frequently do at home, in school, and on your job.

2. What kinds of writing do those employed in your field do regularly?

3. What are several advantages of written communication over oral communication?

4. Based upon your past experiences, what do you find most difficult about having to communicate in writing?

5. Based upon your past experiences, identify as many rules for good writing you can think of.

_____ Poor Written Communication: a Dialogue _____

Supervisor Chen calls two travel agents into the executive office after receiving a telephone call from an irate customer.

CHEN: I was hoping you two could help me to understand what happened to cause our best client, Sam Kendall, to call and scream at me for over half an hour. Do you know that we lost Kendall's business?

LUPE: I handled that booking from a note that Robbie left me regarding Kendall's vacation plans.

ROBBIE: Uh . . . Yeah. I think I took the information from a visit late on a Friday afternoon right before my own week long vacation. I put the note on Lupe's desk before I left for my own two-week vacation hoping that the bookings would be made.

LUPE: Oh yes. I have the note right here. Here it is:

    Sam Kendall, a person with grey hair, wearing red slacks, a blue blazer, and a gold bracelet would like to have a "good time" in Melbourne, in addition to visiting Miami. Kendall will be attending a conference. The dates are March 17th through the 31st.

CHEN: Yes, so what did you do Lupe?

LUPE: I booked Kendall on a flight to Melbourne, Australia, on March 17th. I made reservations at all the hotels with the best discos in the center of the city. Then I booked Kendall on a return flight to Miami, Florida, on the 26th, providing enough time to recover from jet lag. Why? What went wrong?

CHEN: I'll tell you exactly what went wrong. First, the conference was on the 17th through the 20th in Miami. Kendall wanted to go to Miami first but instead missed the conference completely.

ROBBIE: Well, conferences are usually boring anyway.

CHEN: Secondly, Kendall wanted a nice quiet vacation sitting under a palm tree reading a book. A "good time" to Kendall does not include bright lights, big cities, and deafening discos. And finally. . .

ROBBIE: It couldn't have been all that bad. Kendall did get to go to Melbourne.

CHEN: Kendall wanted to go to Melbourne, Florida, *not* Melbourne, Australia! Before realizing what had happened, Kendall was over the Pacific Islands. I hope you can understand how irritating it is for customers to spend time and money going to the wrong place. Robbie, how do you explain yourself for this mess?

ROBBIE: Well . . . I've relocated the trash cans to more convenient places since I've come back, wouldn't you say?

CHEN: Robbie, you're *fired!*

Poor Kendall could have been spared the frustration of ruined travel plans, and Robbie could have been saved the embarrassment of losing a good job had effective writing skills been employed on the job.

Effective Written Communication

As we mentioned earlier, a significant part of your success on a job is dependent upon your ability to communicate effectively with superiors, subordinates, and co-workers. While a majority of your time spent in communication will be devoted to speaking and listening, it is probably safe to assume that your job will require you to communicate in writing as well. Some occupations demand a greater degree of writing skills than others.

Individuals preparing for careers as secretaries or administrative assistants, for instance, are likely to spend a sizable portion of their workday writing letters and memos and taking phone messages. Auto mechanics or office equipment repair personnel may do less writing, as well as different types of writing, but no doubt they will be called upon to prepare customer work orders, write up purchase orders, provide written job estimates, and so on.

Remember, too, that as you advance in your job to positions of increased responsibility, the need for good communication skills, both in speaking and writing, increases as well. Many of the skills that enhance oral communication also contribute to effective written communication. However, while the goal of both effective speaking and writing is *understanding* between sender and receiver, this understanding is often more difficult to achieve in writing.

The employee who seeks to communicate information through the written word does not have the advantages of immediate feedback, facial expression, gestures, and vocal intonation to assist in the sending of a message the way a speaker does. Consequently, the secretary sending a memo or the automotive service technician preparing a work order must make even greater efforts to transmit information accurately, choose words carefully, and arrange ideas logically. The results of unclear written communication can range from apparently minor misunderstandings to more serious consequences, such as the loss of a customer, valuable production time, or money.

Three Questions the Writer Must Address

While the kinds of writing required for occupations varies from simple phone messages to complex reports, the writer must always consider the following questions: What is my subject? What is my purpose? Who is my reader? The answers to these three questions can determine the effectiveness of your communication.

The subject refers to the actual information you wish to convey to the reader. The types of written information you send in your day-to-day communication with superiors, subordinates, and co-workers are as varied as the topics you talk about in office meetings, in the shop, or at the lunchroom table. As a writer, you may notify a distributor about a shipment of defective parts you received, congratulate a co-worker on a recent promotion, or ask your supervisor to call an important customer who has some questions that need answering.

Not only must you keep in mind the subject of your message, you must also have a clear idea of the purpose of your message. Purpose refers to the goal or objective of your communication. In other words, what impact do you wish your message to have upon your reader? Probably most of the messages that are sent and received on the job are intended to inform, instruct, or persuade a reader.

For example, a letter sent by the personnel department announcing the date, time, and location of this year's company picnic is intended to inform. A note you leave for your second shift replacement on how to close out the register at the end of the night is primarily written to instruct. A memo you write to your supervisor stating why you're worthy of a pay raise is largely intended to persuade.

Notice, too, that many times your purposes may overlap. For instance, when you send a letter of application and résumé, you want to persuade an employer that you are the best person for the job. In order to accomplish this, however, you also need to include plenty of information about your job skills, educational background, and character strengths.

Finally, whenever you sit down to write, you need to think about your reader. Too often you may assume that as long as your message is clear to you, it will also be clear to your reader. This assumption is not necessarily correct.

In Chapter 1, we stated that the meanings of words are inside of us rather than in the words themselves. Because of the differences in our backgrounds, no two people are likely to have identical meanings for any word. Consequently, when analyzing your messages, think about whether or not the reader will understand your words, especially if you are using technical words or slang.

No two people have identical
meanings for any word.

Then you need to determine how much information the reader actually needs to know. Sometimes writers may include unnecessary detail, thereby confusing the reader. At other times, writers may be so brief in their messages that the reader is left with many unanswered questions. A good rule of thumb is to imagine that you are the reader, and then ask yourself, "Would I understand this message if I received it?"

Although an understanding of subject, purpose, and reader can contribute to clearer written communication, these factors alone do not necessarily ensure success. Writing is a complex process that involves many different skills from organizing your ideas logically to spelling your words and punctuating your sentences correctly. A significant number of the problems resulting from unclear written communication can be reduced if you keep in mind three important principles of good writing: *Accuracy*, *Clarity*, and *Economy* (abbreviated ACE).

Accuracy

Accuracy in writing occurs when you make sure that you have included *all* of the necessary information and that your information is *correct*.

When a secretary receives a telephone message for a supervisor regarding the rescheduling of an important management meeting, the secretary needs to be certain to get all of the information: who called, when the call was received, what meeting the caller is rescheduling, the date, time, and location of the rescheduled meeting, and so on. An electronic servicing technician is in a similar situation when a customer brings a TV in for repairs. Not only must the technician obtain a complete list of all the customer's complaints, but also the technician must be sure to record those complaints objectively.

Both completeness and correctness in writing can be promoted when you take time to use some of the oral skills you have learned. For example, before you attempt to write a phone message or a customer's order, make sure you fully understand what the sender means. Ask for more information or clarification by using questioning responses if you are the least bit uncertain of the sender's point.

Paraphrasing can be equally effective in promoting understanding. Taking a few extra minutes to restate the sender's message in your own words not only ensures accurate reception of the information but reassures the sender of your interest and concern.

Remember also to separate facts from inferences. All too often we make inferences about the intended meaning of a message, and these inferences may not be accurate. Rather than inferring what the sender may be thinking, feeling, or meaning, use perception checking skills to determine the accuracy of your inferences.

Finally, accuracy in written communication can be enhanced when the mechanics of your written messages are correct. Make sure that your words are spelled correctly and that your sentences are punctuated properly. Misspelled words and missing punctuation may force the reader to guess your intended meaning.

Clarity

Clarity, the second principle of good writing, can be enhanced when you transmit your written messages with the most specific language possible and make sure that your information is logically organized.

In Chapter 3 on "Sending Skills," we discussed the fact that each one of us has different perceptions of the world around us that cause us to interpret information differently. The more *general* or vague you are in sending messages, the greater the likelihood of the receiver misinterpreting your message.

When a clerk typist is given a written job order that reads, "Type this all staff memo on the recent change in employee health benefits as soon as possible," does the writer mean, "Do the job when you're finished with the work you're doing," or "Drop whatever you're doing because this is more important"? The clerk typist will likely make that decision on the basis of past experience, and the interpretation may be incorrect.

The more specific you are in sending messages, the more you reduce the possibility of misinterpretation by the receiver. A message reading, "This all staff memo on changes in employee health benefits needs to be typed by 4:00 p.m. today," is more specific and considerably clearer.

When you are striving to achieve clarity in your writing, you need to pay particular attention to your word choices. The words you use to express your thoughts in writing may range from very general to very specific, as well as anywhere in between these two extremes. To understand this point more fully, examine the following illustration:

creature—animal—domestic animal—cat—Siamese

Notice how the word at the far left is quite general. Creature could refer to almost any living being from an insect to a human. As you move from left to right, the words become increasingly more specific. It is much easier to picture in your mind, for instance, a Siamese cat than a domestic animal.

Most of us tend to be too general in our written communication. We often choose general words with the assumption that the reader will understand our message. However, we also choose general words because it's easier to do. Trying to find more precise language to express our thoughts takes considerably greater time and effort, but this added time and effort are worth it. Communicating ideas specifically reduces the possibility of the reader misinterpreting our meaning.

Clarity is also increased when the information is logically organized. Imagine for a moment that you are trying to assemble a model car or airplane and that the directions are organized randomly rather than step by step. You would probably spend hours just trying to sort through the directions and put them into some kind of logical order before you could even begin the assembling process.

The same holds true for any kind of writing that we do. We have to arrange our ideas in some sort of pattern that will make our message clear to a reader. While there are many different ways to organize ideas in writing, the most common patterns are based on time, space, topic, and problem/solution. We will be looking at each of these patterns in more detail later in the chapter.

Economy

Economy, the third principle of good writing, is achieved when you present essential information to accomplish your purpose in the fewest but most meaningful words possible. Before you can make economical word choices, you should think about your reader's needs. Consider what information your reader is likely to know about your subject and how you may build on this information with added details that are needed for the reader to fully understand your message.

Let's assume you are writing a set of directions on how to construct a letter of complaint to a local manufacturer. The background and experience of the reader will greatly influence the content of your writing. If your reader is an experienced letter writer, you may simply need to identify the nature of the complaint, the desired resolution, and the tone you wish your letter to take. On the other hand, if your reader is an inexperienced letter writer, additional information regarding format, spacing, and copies may be needed.

Although consideration of your reader's needs cannot guarantee understanding between the writer and the reader, these needs can at least help you to determine what to include in your message and what to omit.

Once you have determined the necessary information to include in a message, then you need to select the words that will most effectively convey that information. To a large extent, economy in writing results when you learn to be specific in your word choices. However, occasionally we use more words to express our thoughts when fewer words would have worked just as well, if not better. In the following list, notice how the words in the right column say the same thing as the words in the left column but more economically.

WORDY	**ECONOMICAL**
an excessive amount of	too much
at all times	always
at the present time	now
by means of	by
for the purpose of	for
has the capability of	can
in the event that	if
in the majority of cases	usually
in view of the fact that	since
until such time as	until

The following exercises are designed to give you practice in writing a variety of messages—from taking simple phone messages to writing complex job instructions—*accurately, clearly,* and *economically.* If you do your best to practice and apply these principles to all of your written communications, you are on your way to becoming a writing *ace!*

CHAPTER 4 CHECK UP

Use these key words from the preceding chapter to complete the following sentences.

feedback   increases
accuracy   understanding
clarity   paraphrasing
misinterpretation   economical
speaking   inferences

1. The goal of all effective spoken or written communication is

   Understanding

2. *accuracy* in writing results when you include all of the necessary

   facts.

3. One way to check your understanding of a sender's message before

   putting it into written form is to use ~~clarity~~ *paraphrasing* ,

4. Concrete or specific word choices contribute to ~~paraphrasing~~ *Clarity* in writing.

5. Written messages that are too general frequently result in *misinterpretation*

6. Keeping your written messages brief and to the point makes your writing

   economical

7. Many of the skills of effective *Speaking* also relate to good writing.

8. As you advance on your job, the need for good communication skills

   increases

9. Effective oral communication may be easier to achieve because

   feedback is usually immediate.

10. One way of making sure your writing is accurate is by learning to separate

    inferences from facts.

PART 1—ACCURACY: FINDING THE MISSING INFORMATION WORK SHEET

Accuracy in writing can be achieved when you make sure that you have included all of the necessary information to promote reader understanding of your message. In other words, did you tell the reader everything that needs to be known in order to complete a process, follow a procedure, or respond to a request?

In the following messages, identify what important information the writer failed to include that would have made the message more clearly understood.

EXAMPLE 1

Dear Ms. Johnson:

The shipment of office supplies that our company, Ace Electronics, received from you last week was incomplete.

Could you please inform us when the remaining supplies will be shipped? We need them by the end of the week, or else we shall be forced to complete our order with another supplier.

Sincerely,

Kerry Adams

EXAMPLE 2

MEMO

TO: All Employees

FROM: R. Fredericks, Personnel

DATE: August 22

RE: Parking Regulations

You'll be pleased to know that as a result of the many suggestions we received on how to improve current employee parking regulations, a new policy will be implemented on September 1.

We believe that this new policy will promote easier access to all locations of the plant and thereby decrease arrival and departure times from your work stations.

If you have any questions, don't hesitate to contact me in Personnel.

EXAMPLE 3

Dear Mr. Jacobson:

I wish to be interviewed for the new position that was posted on the employee bulletin board late Thursday morning.

As you know, I have been with the company for over five years, and I believe I am well qualified for the responsibilities this new position requires.

Please let me know about the formal application procedures that I must follow.

Yours truly,

Dale White

EXAMPLE 4

Dear Sir or Madam:

I am writing to reserve a room for Ms. Joanna Weber at your new Westmont Hotel on Fairfax Avenue.

Ms. Weber will be arriving on October 23 for the start of the Management Trainees Seminar being held at the Convention Center.

Kindly confirm this reservation by October 1.

Sincerely,

Tracey Ford

EXAMPLE 5

OPERATION OF THE VCR PLAYBACK UNIT

1. Turn power switch on TV monitor to *on* position.
2. Depress VCR *Power* switch on playback unit.
3. Press *rewind* to rewind cassette tape.
4. After tape is rewound, press *play* button.
5. Adjust volume and focus on TV monitor.

GETTING THE FACTS WORK SHEET

Accuracy in writing is achieved not only when you make sure you have included all of the necessary information for sending clear messages but also when your information or "facts" are correct. As we mentioned earlier, correctness of information can be more readily obtained when you learn to separate the *facts* from your *opinions* (or inferences) and use the verbal skills of perception checking, paraphrasing, and behavior descriptions to verify the information you intend to communicate in writing.

Read each of the following messages only once, and then try to answer the questions that follow without going back to reread the message a second time. We think you'll discover that even immediately after reading a relatively short message, it is not as easy as you may think to recall all of the facts accurately.

Message 1: Accident Report

On Monday, February 23, at 8:10 a.m., a collision occurred in Parking Lot C in front of the physical plant building. A white, 1987 Pontiac Trans-Am had just made a left-hand turn off of Highway G into the employee parking lot and was proceeding north into Lot C when a 1985 red Chevy van entering the lot from the east failed to yield the right of way and hit the Trans-Am broadside on the passenger's compartment. There were no personal injuries, and both drivers reported traveling at about 10 m.p.h. The driver of the van evidently had slowed down upon reaching the yield sign but did not see the driver of the Pontiac approaching due to poor visibility caused by precipitation. There were no other witnesses to the accident.

Questions:

1. What time did the accident occur?
2. In front of which building did the accident occur?
3. What was the weather like when the accident occurred?
4. In what direction was the Pontiac traveling when it was hit?
5. What make and year was the van that hit the Pontiac?

Message 2: Shipping Department

The following parts must be shipped by air freight to Westin Electronics on Friday, March 18:

    12 TX11's at $8.00 each
     5 PC40's at $16.00 each
     8 KB-X's at $7.00 each
    16 TK50's at $2.00 each

The payment for these parts, along with charges for shipping and handling, has already been received, so there is no balance due. Please call Mr. Martin Wilson at 322-9684, extension 236, to notify him of the parts being sent.

Questions:

1. How are these parts to be shipped?
2. How many different types of parts were included in the order?
3. To which company are the parts being shipped?
4. For whom does Mr. Martin Wilson work?
5. On which date are the parts to be shipped?

Message 3: Office Memorandum

I am happy to notify all office personnel of the supervisory training workshops that are scheduled during March, April, and May. The first workshop during the week of March 16–20 is entitled "Learning to Listen Effectively." The second workshop during the week of April 18–22 is entitled "Developing Winning Attitudes on the Job." The third workshop during May 22–26 is entitled "Resolving Conflicts with Assertiveness Skills." All of these workshops will be held on Mondays, Tuesdays, and Wednesdays from 4:00 to 6:00 p.m., with no charge to participants, in Staff Training Room B. Anyone interested in advancing to supervisory positions within the company will find these workshops invaluable. Enrollment is limited to 40 for each workshop, so register early. Registration forms are available from Sandy Marshall in Personnel. Deadline for registration is February 22.

Questions:

1. What three topics are covered during these workshops?
2. Who is encouraged to participate in these workshops?
3. What days of the week and times are scheduled for the workshops?
4. How many employees may enroll in each workshop?
5. What is the deadline for registration?

WRITING ASSIGNMENT 1: REPORTS OF OBSERVATION

To ensure that your written communication is complete and correct, you have to become a good observer. All too often our communication, both written and oral, is based on what we think we heard or saw; we fail to recognize that our perceptions are colored by our past experiences, our moods and feelings, and our physical traits.

Consequently, the messages we send are more often a reflection of our perceptions than of the "facts" themselves, resulting in additions, omissions, or distortions of the information being transmitted.

This writing assignment will require you to use your powers of observation in order to gather and convey information to a reader as accurately as possible. Choose one of the following topics on which to write an observational report.

1. You have experienced the breakdown of a piece of machinery or equipment in your shop or office. Prepare a detailed work order for your supervisor in which you clearly identify what the problem is, when and where the breakdown occurred, and what assistance you're requesting to remedy the problem.

2. You have witnessed an on-the-job injury to a co-worker which occurred in your area. To comply with the company's worker's compensation policy, you must complete an accident report. Indicate what happened, when, where, to whom, and what immediate help was provided for the injured worker.

3. You recently received a complaint from a customer or client regarding a defective product or unsatisfactory service from your company. All customer complaints must be submitted in writing to the customer service department. In your report, identify the customer, the exact nature of the complaint, the date and time the complaint was made, and the resolution the customer is seeking.

WORD LADDER EXERCISE

In any written communication, whether it be a work order, a set of instructions, a memorandum, or a letter of application, choose the most specific words possible in order to increase the likelihood of your reader understanding your message exactly as you intended it.

This exercise provides you with an opportunity to practice selecting specific words for your written communications. Divide into groups with four or five other students, and select one of the sets of words below (A, B, or C). For each word in a given set, construct a five rung ladder, making each new word you select more specific than the word on the rung above it. The last word on your ladder should be the most specific word of the group. A sample ladder is provided for you.

Sample Ladder

APPLIANCE

1. Home appliance
2. Kitchen appliance
3. Oven
4. Microwave oven
5. Riggs roaster microwave

A	B	C
EDUCATION	**COMPETITION**	**INSTITUTION**
1. _____	1. _____	1. _____
2. _____	2. _____	2. _____
3. _____	3. _____	3. _____
4. _____	4. _____	4. _____
5. _____	5. _____	5. _____
MECHANISM	**TRANSACTION**	**ATHLETICS**
1. _____	1. _____	1. _____
2. _____	2. _____	2. _____
3. _____	3. _____	3. _____
4. _____	4. _____	4. _____
5. _____	5. _____	5. _____

APPAREL	SERVICE	INDUSTRY
1. _____	1. _____	1. _____
2. _____	2. _____	2. _____
3. _____	3. _____	3. _____
4. _____	4. _____	4. _____
5. _____	5. _____	5. _____

WRITING ASSIGNMENT 2: INSTRUCTION WRITING

One of the most precise forms of writing an employee can do is preparing a set of written instructions that a reader must be able to follow with complete understanding. Examples of instructional writing can range from a simple follow-up note on a telephone message received to a highly detailed explanation about the operation of a complex piece of machinery.

Regardless of what kind of instructions you write on the job, they should be so complete and correct that a reader is able to follow them exactly without wondering, "What did the writer mean?"

Here are a few suggestions that will enable you to convey instructional information effectively to your reader:

1. Identify the significance or importance of the instructions for your reader. For example, "These instructions explain how to complete the new tax withholding form so the correct deductions can be made from your paycheck."

2. Use simple terms. If you must include technical language or "jargon," be sure you provide definitions the reader will understand.

3. Number your steps and include only one task per step. Avoid asking the reader to do two or more tasks at one time.

4. Make sure you've included all of the necessary information; your reader won't be able to complete the instructions correctly if necessary details are missing.

5. Make sure your steps are chronologically arranged. Even one step out of order can make your instructions impossible to follow.

6. Eliminate unnecessary use of the pronoun "you." Begin each step with an action verb instead. Rather than writing "First you depress the power switch," simply say "Depress power switch." The latter approach is less wordy and focuses on the action you want your reader to take.

7. Make your reader aware of any precautions. For example, "*Caution:* Failure to engage the safety valve may result in serious injury to the operator of this machine."

Keeping in mind these seven suggestions, choose a subject from the following list (or choose one of your own), and write your own set of instructions.

TOPICS

How to operate a switchboard

How to operate a word processor

How to administer emergency first aid for a specific injury

How to develop an office filing system

How to type a memo

How to take a product inventory

How to complete an income tax form

How to balance a checkbook

How to tune a car engine

How to jump start a stalled car

How to prepare a budget
How to winterize a car
How to prepare for a job interview
How to purchase a home
How to plan a trip overseas

PART 3—ECONOMY: ELIMINATING UNNECESSARY WORDS EXERCISE

The final characteristic of effective written communication is *economy*. Economic writing requires the concise use of language without sacrificing clarity or accuracy. Wordiness, excessive repetition, and unnecessary information all must be avoided. Economic word choices provide the reader with information that can be clearly and quickly understood.

The following exercises will help you to write more economically. Rewrite the following sentences by eliminating unnecessary wording.

Example: The steps in the procedure to learn how to operate the automatic computing system should be carefully read and understood in order to prevent costly mistakes that could result in expensive losses to the company.

Rewrite: To avoid costly mistakes, learn how to use the automatic computing system.

1. Forms completed yesterday, before today's changes, will be treated and processed as if they had been completed today after the aforesaid changes.

2. Prompt payment of unpaid balances on outstanding bills will be greatly appreciated by those who continue to process your accounts.

3. Each and every one of the individual persons surveyed agreed with the consensus that consumer prices were beyond what average citizens could be expected to pay based on their personal income earnings.

4. After repeatedly requesting several times the need for replacement technicians in the repair department to fix valuable broken equipment that has malfunctioned, we have decided to voice our frustration by filing a grievance.

5. Customers who have purchased defective or faulty goods are not allowed nor permitted to return them for a refund or an exchange without their sales receipt or some proof of purchase.

6. Overall, the decision to revise the schedule was due to basic, underlying changes that we believe needed to be made as a result of the in-depth, lengthy study and analysis of the needs of the consumers as a whole.

7. The use of the "fifo" method would clearly liminate questionable inventories that are of uncertain value.

8. Identical angles of sixty degrees and sixty degrees c n be expected to intersect when directly adjacent to each other.

9. As observed and reported by the supervisor investigating the al   ed act of negligence, these acts are very often unreported, if mentioned a   ll.

10. Yesterday, at 3:00 p.m., just as the first shift was ending and getting off work, Ronnie commended the crew of employees about their outstanding production record they had set this week.

THERE IS . . . THERE ARE WORK SHEET

"There are" and "there is" both add unnecessary words to your writing and should be avoided whenever possible. Simply eliminate these words, and begin the sentence with whatever would follow one of these culprits. For example, "There are four items that I need to order this month," could easily become, "Four items need ordering this month." The economy is obvious.

Revise these sentences to show more active subjects and to eliminate the wordiness.

1. There is this noise which is heard periodically from the control panel.

2. When there are 11 responses from the customers, there are enough to begin the tour.

3. There were all but one of the inspected valves waiting to be packaged on the supervisor's desk.

4. There are always three steps that must be performed in this order.

5. If there are no more applicants for the job, then there are only two who qualify.

6. There are reservations for the entire committee ordered from the Nelson Agency.

7. There are several problems in meeting the proposed deadlines.

8. After there is sufficient clearance to guarantee the safety of the lifting mechanism, the boom may be lowered.

9. There are many negligent and costly errors occurring early this season.

10. When there are three more experienced crew members to join us, there will be less work for all of us to do.

WRITING ASSIGNMENT 3: LETTER WRITING

Your written communication links you to other employees and represents you and your company to the rest of the business world. Demonstrate that you have mastered accuracy, clarity, and economy by writing documents that present precise, necessary information, logically organized, using specific and efficient word choices.

Type a standard business letter which addresses a specific concern. Use the letter format found in Chapter 5 under "Letter of Application." Consider the following as possible subjects:

1. Request information about a conference or meeting. Be sure to ask about location, date, time, agenda, accommodations, registration fees, and the name of the conference organizer for additional information.
2. Request information about repair procedures for a particular machine. Be sure to identify the model number of the machine; describe the nature of the problem; and ask for specific directions to correct the problem.
3. Complain about nonpayment of an insurance claim. State when the claim was submitted, the nature of the claim, policy, and identification numbers; refer to other correspondence related to the claim and request payment.
4. Explain a change in company policy or procedure. Mention what specific policy or procedure is being referred to; specify the change being made and the reason why; state for whom the change is intended and when it will be implemented.

Chapter 5

EMPLOYABILITY SKILLS

―――― Preview Questions ――――――――――――――――――――――

1. What problems have you experienced when seeking and applying for employment?

2. What role do effective listening and speaking skills play in helping you to get and keep a job?

3. What characteristics about applicants do you feel employers/interviewers are most interested in?

4. Where would you go to find out information about a specific career?

5. What is a résumé? What would you do if you had to write one?

6. What do you believe are the characteristics of a good job application?

7. Based on job interviews that you've had, list some reasons why you were hired or not hired.

———— An Unusual Job Interview: a Dialogue ————————————————————————

Jamie meets with Supervisor Cook to be interviewed for a job. The following interaction occurs in Cook's office:

COOK: So why are you applying for this job?
JAMIE: Huh? I don't know. I need the money, I guess.
COOK: What special skills do you have to offer this company?
JAMIE: Well, I'm real good at partying and having a good time.
COOK: That's enough. What things are you looking for in a satisfying job?
JAMIE: Vacation time . . . and more vacation time!
COOK: Do you know what you want out of life?
JAMIE: Sure; good times!
COOK: Do you even know what a tool and die maker does?
JAMIE: Sure. Tools and dies, right?
COOK: What do you know about this company?
JAMIE: Well, I know you're open from 8:00 a.m. to 5:00 p.m. What else does a worker need to know?
COOK: Do you know what we do here?
JAMIE: Heck, if I knew that, I already would've worked here. I'm willing to learn what you do.
COOK: Your application is sloppy and incomplete. You don't have a résumé.
JAMIE: A what?
COOK: And you look like you're dressed for the sideshow of a carnival! Why should I hire you?
JAMIE: Because my parents own the company!
COOK: You're hired! See you first thing Monday morning.
JAMIE: Well, to tell you the truth, Cookie, I like to sleep late, and Monday mornings are the pits. What if I show up by noon?

Unless you're in Jamie's shoes, and far too few of us are, you will need to be concerned about all aspects of the employment process. It is important that you know what you want from an occupation, what you have to offer a company, what the company needs from you, and how to communicate that you and the available position are a match made in heaven!

Unfortunately, this is easier said than done. Thinking about what you want out of life and getting a job that is compatible with those needs is a difficult and time-consuming process. Unless you are willing to work, work, work, you may as well resign yourself to boring jobs with insufficient reward.

Thinking about what you want from life and employment is no simple task. Richard Bolles, a noted career expert, maintains that the first twenty to thirty hours of job hunting should be spent at home doing career/self exploration "homework."[1]

Likewise, the process of finding employment takes considerable time and effort. The average time it takes to find employment is 115 days—nearly four months! You can benefit by using this time to do the research necessary to find those occupations with favorable present and future employment prospects which are also compatible with your interests and needs.

The actual job hunt will involve your active efforts and a desire for near perfection. The job interview is the single most important activity that will determine whether or not you'll get the job. However, knowing how to write effective résumés, letters of application, follow-up letters, and how to fill out application forms are also important in the overall job hunt scheme.

Finally, after such long, difficult work finding the right job, you'll need to have good interpersonal skills to keep it. This is also a challenging task since, according to Robert Bolton in his book *People Skills*, 80 percent of employment

[1]Richard N. Bolles, What Color Is Your Parachute? (Berkeley: Ten Speed Press, 1985) p. 46.

terminations are related to an inability to get along with others and not an inability to do the job.[2]

We believe there are four major steps to reaching and maintaining your career goals:

Step 1: Choosing the right career.
Step 2: Choosing a specific occupation.
Step 3: Getting employed.
Step 4: Maintaining employment satisfaction.

Within each of these areas, several minor steps will help you attain the major goals outlined above. Each step will be discussed in detail with activities provided to help you through the employment process.

Step 1: Choosing the Right Career

Before we begin our discussion of choosing the right career, let us define what is meant by the term "career" and see how it differs from two other closely related words: occupation and job.

Your career is your general profession, usually seen as a lifelong pursuit (the mechanical field, the electronics field, the business occupations field, etc.). Your occupation is the specific title of your profession (industrial machine mechanic, television and radio technician, clerk typist, etc.). Your job, as used here, is the exact title, duties, and location of your work (computer numerical control technician at Acme Industrial, grade 7). The major activity associated with choosing a career is self-exploration. In fact, many noted career experts maintain that 90 percent of finding a job is knowing what you want from a career.

The process of knowing yourself is not an easy one. You know your name, age, height, weight, etc. But this process involves more than an awareness of your vital statistics. Knowing yourself requires thinking about what you want out of life (goals), what's important to you (values), what you enjoy doing (interests), and what abilities you have to offer a prospective employer (skills and achievements).

Knowing yourself involves finding a career that is compatible with your goals, values, interests, and skills. Generally, the more consistent these factors are with your work, the greater will be your degree of employment satisfaction. After all, almost one-third of your life will be spent in employment, and you may as well choose a career you will enjoy.

It might be interesting to note that 80 percent of all workers label themselves as underemployed (doing work that does not use their full potential). Most likely, they have haphazardly chosen careers, taking jobs that happened to open up, rather than carefully planning for their future.

You may feel that exploring career choices is a waste of time because you've already chosen a career and may be near completion of a vocational program. Keep in mind that the average American will make seven occupation or job changes in life, and with the modernization of our society, the future holds probably even more change. Gone are the days of the lifelong, single job worker.

Interviewers may ask you personal questions that directly relate to know-

[2]Robert Bolton, Ph.D., People Skills (Englewood Cliffs, NJ: Prentice Hall, 1979) p. 7.

Knowing yourself involves more
than an awareness of your
vital statistics.

ing yourself such as, "What special skills set you apart from other applicants?" or they may ask questions that indirectly relate to your career such as, "At school, what courses did you like best? Least? Why?"

Interviewers want to know "who you are." Of the 81 most frequently asked questions in an interview, as reported by 92 companies to Frank Endicott, Director of Placement at Northwestern University, 65 percent of the questions are related to "who you are.[3]" Examples include "Where do you expect to be five years from now? What, in your opinion, is the value of your vocational education? What are your pet peeves?" If you have a clear picture of "who you are" in advance, chances are you can answer questions like these more completely and confidently.

Discovering "who you are" can be simplified by asking yourself whether you prefer to work with people, information, or machines, since most occupations require a greater emphasis in one of these areas. For example, an auto mechanic and administrative assistant may work primarily with machines and information; whereas, the hospitality manager or medical assistant may work mainly with people. This general perspective provides a valuable way to begin the process of self-exploration.

[3]Frank S. Endicott, "Making The Most Of Your Job Interview," A New York Life Insurance Company pamphlet (Evanston, IL: Placement Center, Northwestern University).

Another more specific guide to knowing "who you are" was developed by John L. Holland, Ph.D. His RIASEC model involves typecasting yourself in one of the following categories:[4]

Realistic—having athletic or mechanical ability.

Investigative—preferring to observe, learn, analyze, and solve problems.

Artistic—having intuition, imagination, and/or creativity.

Social—preferring to work with people to train/cure.

Enterprising—working with people but for economic gain.

Clerical—working with numbers, data, and following instructions.

Holland believes that ranking the three characteristics most typical of you gives an important indication of your personality. Questionnaires have been developed by Holland to help identify your personality type. One such questionnaire is the *The Self Directed Search*[5] which can be used with *The Occupations Finder* to determine your most appropriate career choices using the RIASEC categories. Many school counselors use this system or can direct you in finding these resources.

Resources are provided in this text to help you answer the questions, "who am I, what kind of work do I want, and what kind of work am I capable of?" Begin by identifying your *interests*; career satisfaction is related to allowing you time to do the things you enjoy doing, both on and off the job. Next, focus on your abilities by listing your *achievements*. Further, you will discover specific abilities through defining your technical, personal, and life *skills*. Then you identify *work values* to give an indication of what is important to you in the career you choose. Finally, determine your long- and short-term *goals* to give you an idea of the direction you want to pursue.

With this information, you can begin to find out about occupations that are compatible with your personality. Real job satisfaction comes from finding work that matches your goals, values, abilities, and interests.

Again, knowing yourself is essential for discovering what is important to you and for finding a satisfying occupation. Beyond this, you have the bonus of preparing yourself to answer questions from interviewers relative to "who you are." Co-workers and employers, after all, want to know "who you are" since they will have to work with you.

Interests

Professional angler? Professional wine taster? Professional billiards player? Does that sound like the kind of job you would like to have? Although most of us can't get paid for doing what we enjoy most, a few people are fortunate and creative enough to find ways to turn active interests into full-time careers.

The majority of us have to be content with finding careers that give us the flexibility to engage our interests, either indirectly on the job or directly off the job. In fact, there is a logical connection between our degree of career satisfaction and the time we are allowed to participate in our areas of active interest.

Obviously, the auto mechanic who enjoys working on cars, both as a hobby and for a living, will experience a high degree of worker satisfaction. The

[4]John L. Holland, Ph.D., "The Self Directed Search" (Palo Alto, CA: Consulting Psychological Press, 1977).

[5]*Ibid.*

secretary who likes international travel but who does not have enough time off to do so will be resentful about having chosen a field that gives minimal opportunity for personal enjoyment. Employees need to choose occupations that enable them to pursue their interests.

Many employers will ask about your interests during job interviews. Questions frequently asked include: How do you spend your free time? How do you spend your vacations? What are your hobbies? What did you like about school or past jobs? All of these questions are ways of finding out about your interests and of providing interviewers with a clear picture of those you do well.

How you spend your free time gives some clue about what you're interested in. When identifying your interests, consider hobbies, enjoyable aspects of past or present jobs, classes taken that were enjoyable, people you're with and activities you do together, topics you like to talk about or listen to, achievements, and volunteer activities.

Complete the following *interest inventory* work sheet to help you to identify your interests and patterns in those interests. Use this information to help choose a career that will give you maximum opportunity to pursue your interests. Review this inventory before a job interview in order to answer employer questions about your personal interests.

INTEREST INVENTORY WORK SHEET

List your ten most important interests; then complete the interests questionnaire that follows.

My Most Important Interests Are:

1.

2.

3.

4.

5.

6.

7.

8.

9.

10.

INTEREST QUESTIONNAIRE WORK SHEET

1. What patterns can you see in the interests that you have identified? Consider the following: alone or with others, indoors or outdoors, seasonal or year-round, relaxing and passive or tense and active, cooperative or competitive, inexpensive or expensive, equipment required or not, etc.

2. Would you be willing to change professions if you could not pursue your interests? Why or why not?

3. To what extent do you believe your chosen occupation will allow you to participate in your identified interests? What might you do to increase the chances of participating in your interest areas?

4. If an employer asked, "What do you do during your free time," how would you respond?

Achievements

Coming out of the interview at the Remax Corporation, Lonnie kept saying, "I blew it! I know I blew it." Frustration was growing by the moment. Lonnie was qualified for the position and would make a good employee. But when the interviewer asked about personal accomplishments, Lonnie choked.

Lonnie kept hearing over and over again, "Tell me, Lonnie, what have you done? What are some of your accomplishments?" Lonnie wanted to have done something, indeed anything, great. Even claiming one mediocre accomplishment would have been better than the silence that Lonnie had for a response.

Like many job applicants, Lonnie's technical skills are excellent. The competencies acquired at school and at work make Lonnie a well-qualified applicant. However, problems in identifying and communicating these accomplishments to an employer prevented Lonnie from interviewing successfully.

When your accomplishments are not national headlines, you may find it hard to get excited about what you have done. Even though you consider yourself a good technician, you might get uncomfortably modest about your achievements.

The work sheet that follows is designed to help you review your accomplishments and become confident when talking about them. First, you will be asked to review the successes that you have had in different areas of your life. Next, you will participate in an exercise talking about those achievements. Both are designed to prepare you for an interviewer's questions so that you may better sell yourself.

The first step in this process is to review your accomplishments. Richard Irish in his book *Go Hire Yourself an Employer* suggests that this exercise should take three days.[6] We hope to do it in less time, but it may take some time and effort to recall those moments in your life when you felt fulfilled.

Recount that sense of satisfaction which usually follows an accomplishment. Try to recall what you did when you have experienced feelings of pride, satisfaction, or fulfillment. List ten of these achievements on the following work sheet. Use these questions as starters if you need to:

Have you been successful in team sports, bands, clubs, etc.?

Have you earned honors at school or at work?

Have you participated in competition of some sort?

What have you rebuilt, made, or repaired?

Do you have any inventions?

Have you written any articles for publication?

Do you work well with a variety of people?

What work have you done that you are most proud of?

Are you a person that people can count on to organize or expedite a project?

Have you done any risky yet successful adventures (sky diving, mountain climbing, solo singing, etc.)?

Have you done anything very few people can say that they've done?

Have you raised any animals or trained pets?

Have you made public presentations before a group of people?

[6]Richard K. Irish, Go Hire Yourself An Employer (New York: Anchor Press, 1978) p. 29.

ACHIEVEMENT INVENTORY WORK SHEET

List your top ten achievements. Be specific and give concrete examples.

My Personal Achievements

1. I accomplished a 4.0 for the second quarter of freshman college. I have maintained a 3.6.

2. I was honored with being named employee of the month twice at Arbys.

3. I received an honorable mention in the 9th grade English Scholarship team, in which we competed with other schools.

4. Won 2nd place in poetry contest at school. 2nd place in art contest.

5. Won 3rd place in junior high "Olympics" — high jump.

6. Accomplished attending college after one year of working after high school.

7. Accomplished myself as a more open + outgoing person. My previous positions account for this.

8.

9.

10.

PERSONALITY TRAITS WORK SHEET

Now that you have your list, look for trends or themes that show your personality traits, such as "I am eager, cooperative, creative, dependable, etc." Determine five personality traits that you have and find at least one example from your list of achievements to support each trait. This information will be shared with the class or in small groups. It may sound like this: "I'm inventive; one of my inventions is a release for a compound bow. It enables the shooter to release the string more comfortably and with greater accuracy. I've also invented my own tree stand."

If you can't come up with five personality traits, you'll have to read your entire list of achievements to the class and have the class offer five traits that suit you. This exercise is intended to prepare you for talking about yourself so that you can both describe yourself to the employer and give concrete examples of your successes.

My Personality Traits; Examples From My List of Achievements

1. I'm determined; I've had to work very hard to attend college. I worked for a year before attending college and I'm working after school now.

2. I'm trustworthy; I had a store key at Arby's and I wasn't a manager.

3. I'm adaptable; my schedule this year offers no free time & not much sleep. Before this, I had an easy schedule with plenty of spare time.

4. I'm intelligent; I've achieved a 4.0 in college & have maintained a 3.6.

5. I'm friendly; the job positions I have held account for this — I was really shy & was forced to be open & outgoing. I enjoy it.

Skills: Technical, Personal, Life

To decide what type of work you want, you must examine yourself and ask, "What do I have to offer an employer?" That is, what skills, assets, and/or attributes do you possess that an employer would desire in a candidate for a particular position? After all, an employer's main concern is what you have to offer as an employee.

To answer the above question, three categories of skills must be examined. First, what *technical* skills do you have? These job related skills include those you've learned and practiced in past jobs or in an educational setting. Some examples might include reading blueprints, operating a computer, or using a word processor. Remember that just because you've acquired these job related skills through years of training and experience, they do not guarantee you employment.

Personal skills are related to what others say and like about you. These skills deal with your ability to get along with others: co-workers, supervisors, customers, employers, etc. For example, you might be friendly, cooperative, and helpful.

Finally, *life* skills play an important role in an employer's hiring decisions. Though not formally a part of the job requirements, life skills set you apart from other applicants. Examples of life skills include an ability to coach a softball team, to raise children, or to plant a garden. Hobbies and outside activities are typical ways of developing these skills. The skills gained through these experiences say something about your ability to organize people and materials, relate to others, and express your creativity.

Many applicants have the appropriate technical skills. The skills that distinguish one candidate from another are personal and life skills. For example, a travel agency may hire you over other applicants because you speak foreign languages, especially if the agency makes a lot of international reservations. In this sense, personal and life skills may be more important in getting a job than technical skills.

The following assignments are designed to help you identify your skills in all three areas: technical, personal, and life.

TECHNICAL SKILLS WORK SHEET

List five dominant, work related skills that you've attained at this point in your training. Give an example of something you've done that clearly demonstrates you have this skill. (If you get stuck, you may want to use the checklist of 250 verbs that follows in the life skills area.)

Example: Designed. Designed a safe, economical storage system for preserving computer software.

1. Communicated. My communication skills are great. I've had to deal with customers, supervisors, and peers in my communication oriented jobs.

2. Devised. Devised a sales promotion portfolio in which I planned & budgeted a special event.

3. Acted. Acted in dramatic performance This shows my memorization and adaptability skills.

4. Trained. Trained many new employees on job specifics.

5.

PERSONAL SKILLS WORK SHEET

The following list contains adjectives related to personal skills. Circle ten adjectives that describe you. Then underline five adjectives that most clearly show "who you are." Give a specific example of why you would describe yourself in this way. Write your answers in the space provided under the list.

Example: Calm. A fire started in the kitchen of our house, and I calmly put it out.

Intelligent	Efficient	Disciplined
Emotionally stable	Energetic	Decisionmaker
Accepting	Fair	Alert
Adaptable	Outgoing	Commitment
Ambitious	Gentle	to grow
Brave	Sensitive	Curious
Calm	Giving	Cooperative
Carefree	Helpful	Diplomatic
Likeable	Idealistic	Empathetic
Warm	Independent	Enthusiastic
Open-minded	Lively	Expressive
Contented	Logical	Firm
Friendly	Modest	Good judge
Mature	Organized	Understanding
Wise	Patient	Witty
Attractive	Perceptive	Dynamic
Assertive	Precise	Initiative
Honest	Progressive	Loyal
Conscientious	Proud	Optimistic
Dependable	Realistic	Poised
Caring	Reflective	Polite
Happy	Respectable	Resourceful
Confident	Spontaneous	Self-control
Critical	Tactful	Tidy
Determined	Trustworthy	Versatile
Dignified	Zestful	Generous

1. Intelligent. My grades in school show this. High school: A's + B's. College: 3.6-4.0.

2. ADaptable. 1990 schedule. Had to adapt to little or no sleep plus an abundance of stress. I'm used to plenty of sleep.

3. Determined. I'm determined to get my education & to achieve a job I'll be happy with. 1990 schedule of work & school.

4. Trustworthy. I was only a cashier at Arby's, yet they trusted me with a key to the store.

5. Friendly. My previous job experiences relied on my friendliness — I was in direct contact with the public (customer).

LIFE SKILLS WORK SHEET

The following list contains some verbs describing various life skills compiled by R. N. Bolles in his booklet "Your Career."[7] Underline your ten best, most satisfying skills. When you have finished, circle the five verbs that you feel best describe you. Write your circled words at the end of this list, and include a real example of something you've done that shows you clearly have this skill.

Example: Painted. Painted the complete interior and exterior of my parents' home in two weeks during the summer. Received many compliments.

Achieved	Determined	Increased	Planned
Acted	Developed	Influenced	Played
Adapted	Devised	Informed	Predicted
Addressed	Diagnosed	Inspected	Prepared
Administered	Directed	Inspired	Prescribed
Advised	Discovered	Installed	Presented
Analyzed	Displayed	Instituted	Printed
Anticipated	Disproved	Instructed	Problem solved
Arbitrated	Distributed	Integrated	Processed
Ascertained	Diverted	Interviewed	Produced
Assembled	Empathized	Interpreted	Programmed
Assessed	Enforced	Invented	Protected
Attained	Established	Inventoried	Promoted
Audited	Estimated	Investigated	Provided
Arranged	Evaluated	Judged	Publicized
Budgeted	Examined	Kept	Purchased
Built	Explained	Lead	Questioned
Calculated	Expanded	Learned	Raised
Charted	Experimented	Manipulated	Read
Checked	Expressed	Mediated	Realized
Classified	Extracted	Memorized	Reasoned
Coached	Filed	Mentored	Received
Collected	Financed	Met	Reconciled
Communicated	Fixed	Modeled	Recorded
Compiled	Followed	Monitored	Recruited
Completed	Formulated	Motivated	Rehabilitated
Composed	Founded	Navigated	Reduced
Computed	Gathered	Negotiated	Related
Conceptualized	Gave	Observed	Resolved
Conducted	Generated	Obtained	Responded
Consolidated	Got	Offered	Restored
Constructed	Guided	Operated	Retrieved
Conserved	Had responsibility for	Ordered	Reviewed
Controlled	Handled	Organized	Risked
Coordinated	Headed	Originated	Sang
Copied	Hypothesized	Oversaw	Scheduled
Counseled	Identified	Painted	Selected
Defined	Illustrated	Perceived	Sensed
Delivered	Imagined	Performed	Separated
Designed	Implemented	Persuaded	Served
Detailed	Improved	Photographed	Set
Detected	Improvised	Piloted	Set-up

[7]Richard N. Bolles, "Your Career" (Chicago: Success Unlimited Inc., 1982) p. 8A.

Sewed	Summarized	Tended	Tutored
Shaped	Supervised	Tested and proved	Typed
Shared	Supplied	Told	Umpired
Showed	Symbolized	Trained	Understood
Sketched	Synergized	Transcribed	Undertook
Sold	Synthesized	Translated	Unified
Solved	Systematized	Treated	United
Sorted	Talked	Traveled	Used
Spoke	Taught	Troubleshoot	Utilized
Studied	Team built		

1. Determined. I worked a full year after high school to get enough money for college. Now, I work & go to school.

2. Inventoried. Had some experience in this by the Macy's Inventory job.

3. Memorized. Able to memorize — I was in a drama class and performed in front of the school.

4. Had responsibility for. At Arby's, responsible for food preparation (accuracy & timing). I had a store key & was not a member of management.

5. Achieved. 4.0 in college. Scholarship team in high school — honorable mention in competition.

Work Values

Like many people, you probably have never thought about what you value most. Yet values play a strong role in the decisions you make about your everyday life. Your values play an essential role in career choices, career decisions, and career satisfaction.

Your values are those standards of good/bad and right/wrong by which you make personal judgments. Values are a matter of degree, with some values being more important than others. Values are usually long lasting and can be very specifically identified. When you become more aware of the unseen forces which guide your life, you can make more conscious and effective decisions about which direction you plan to pursue.

For example, if you value security in a job position, you would probably prefer a job that offers full time, year round employment, regardless of economic conditions. Likewise, if you value high financial rewards, taking a good paying seasonal job (such as working in a winter resort) would probably bring a significant degree of satisfaction.

The following activity will help you know what you value and how to rank those values so you can begin seeking a career that is consistent with your values. Remember, the greater the degree of compatibility of values with an occupation, the greater the level of job satisfaction.

WORK VALUES RATING SHEET EXERCISE

The following list describes "satisfiers" that people obtain from their occupation. Rate the degree to which each of these satisfiers is important to you using the following scale.

5—very important
4—mostly important
3—neither important nor unimportant
2—mostly unimportant
1—not important at all

4   1. Financial reward—a good salary, and/or healthy benefits or perks.

5   2. Flexibility/variation—the opportunity to do different tasks; not the same thing day in and out.

5   3. Creativity—the opportunity to use your imagination to solve problems or to initiate new ideas.

4   4. Security—the knowledge of future employment no matter what the economic conditions.

5   5. Excitement/challenge—intellectually and/or physically demanding, yet also stimulating.

4   6. Relationships—the opportunity to work with friendly people in a setting that emphasizes the value of people and encourages friendships.

3   7. Independence—the opportunity to work on your own in as many ways as possible, being your own boss.

3   8. Helping others/society—working for the betterment of the lives of those who are in some way disadvantaged.

4   9. Advancement potential—the opportunity to move up within the company to better positions.

3   10. Status/recognition—being seen as a leader in the community and having others seek your advice.

5   11. Sense of accomplishment—feeling proud about the end product and feeling you've accomplished something meaningful.

2   12. Responsibility/power—making important decisions and being accountable for success/failure.

4   13. Location of employment—situated in an area you feel comfortable with and providing you with an opportunity to enjoy your kind of life.

4   14. Physical/psychological health—an environment relatively free from danger to one's physical health and/or mental state.

_5_ **15.** Growth potential—the opportunity to learn new things and expand one's level of awareness and abilities.

_3_ **16.** Time off—work the standard hours with sufficient time off during the week and for vacations.

_3_ **17.** Precision—desire work requiring exactness and accuracy in whatever job tasks are given.

_3_ **18.** Competitiveness—the opportunity to have work matched against that of others.

_4_ **19.** Cooperation—work in an environment where working together is important.

_4_ **20.** Family happiness—work provides well-being for you and your loved ones.

_5_ **21.** Inner harmony—a feeling of oneness, happiness, and contentment.

_5_ **22.** Integrity—an opportunity to maintain your own personal standards and values.

_4_ **23.** Loyalty—demonstrating long-term commitment to a product or a company.

_3_ **24.** Order—working in an environment where things are done in a set way without deviation.

_5_ **25.** Pleasure—work provides much enjoyment and happiness.

_5_ **26.** Wisdom—includes opportunities to learn and grow in knowledge.

WORK VALUES SUMMARY WORK SHEET

Review the values identified in the previous exercise by completing the following work sheet. List your three most important work values in the category called "essential." These values must exist if you are to accept a job. The next category contains the "bonus" values, those three values that are not essential but are important to your career and job satisfaction. Finally, list the "avoidance" values, those three values which would significantly reduce your satisfaction. When finished, answer the questions that follow about your work values.

Work Value Essentials

1.

2.

3.

Work Value Bonuses

1.

2.

3.

Work Values to Avoid

1.

2.

3.

DISCUSSION QUESTIONS

1. What makes the three "essential" values you selected most important to you?

2. How does the occupational area you've chosen meet these essential values?

3. If your current occupation will not allow you to meet those important values, would you be able to gain them in another occupation? If so, what kind of occupations do you imagine would be most compatible with your values?

4. If an employer asked, "What do you value most in a job?" what would you say?

Goal Setting

One of the most important and yet frequently overlooked steps to achieving career satisfaction is the establishment of life *goals*. Simply defined, goals are specific objectives that you desire to attain. Setting goals for yourself and then working toward them give your life direction and meaning. When those goals are ultimately reached, you are rewarded by a sense of personal accomplishment.

Several guidelines for goal setting should be observed before you actually begin to identify your life goals.

1. Goals can be long-term and/or short-term. Long-term goals take a considerable length of time to achieve, perhaps even a lifetime. An example of a long-term goal is your hope to someday own and operate a successful tool company or collection agency. Although reaching long-term goals may seem far off in the future, these goals provide a target to strive for and thereby channel your other career efforts in a specific direction.

   Short-term goals, as the name implies, represent objectives that are likely to be attained in the immediate future. For instance, one of your short-term goals might be to secure employment as an appliance servicing technician with a highly reputable company in your own community. You should aim to have your short-term goals serve as stepping stones to your long-term goals.

2. Goals should be specific rather than general. Specific or concrete goals are more easily attainable than those which are too general. Instead of saying, for example, that you want to secure a job in a field that pays a high salary, it would be more effective to indicate the specific salary you want.

3. Keep your goals realistic and attainable. It is not only impractical but frustrating as well to set goals for yourself that are almost impossible to reach. In order to determine the practicality of your goals, you should be honest in assessing your interests, skills, and values to see if they match the goals you've set.

4. Remain open to the possibility of changing your goals. As you gain more experience in life and on your job, you may find that your goals change.

   Perhaps one of your long-term goals is to manage a motel of your own. After several years of working in the field and observing the responsibilities of owning a business, you may find that being an owner is not as appealing to you as it once was. In such situations, your most logical alternative would be to reassess your goals and move in a direction that offers you greater potential job satisfaction.

5. Own your goals. You should not try to reach goals simply because others have set them for you. Becoming a small engine repair technician because your parents want you to, even though you would actually prefer to work with animals at a local veterinary clinic, would be unsatisfying at best.

   One method of identifying long-term goals that are important to you is to envision yourself at the end of your life. Try to imagine what you would have hoped to have accomplished as you look back. Give some careful thought to this process, and then complete the following Long-Term Goals Inventory.

LONG-TERM GOALS INVENTORY WORK SHEET

As you look at the figure on page 145, you will notice categories in which you will establish your goals. The circle in the center of the inventory represents your career choice.

Two reasons make the career circle the focal point of this inventory. First, you will undoubtedly spend the greatest portion of your waking hours engaged in work. Second, since your career represents one of the most important life decisions you will make, career goals can have a significant impact on the types of goals that you set for yourself in the other four categories.

For example, if you discover that as a result of your long-term goal you will be required to spend more hours working alone than with others, you may find it necessary to establish meaningful relationships outside of your work. Indicate this fact in the social circle of the inventory.

Remember, that if you establish your career goals thoughtfully, in view of your interests, values, and skills, you increase the likelihood of your career goals contributing to and enhancing the other four areas in your life listed on the inventory.

Before you complete the inventory, read the following brief explanations:

CAREER: Occupational or job related objectives, such as positions, companies, responsibilities you wish to have, etc.

PERSONAL: Objectives for "inner growth," such as character and personality development, religious or spiritual goals, etc.

SOCIAL: Relationships with others, such as with family and friends, community involvement, clubs and organizations, etc.

EDUCATIONAL: Academic achievement, such as specialized training, self-study, apprenticeships, etc.

PHYSICAL: Health and fitness, such as exercise, nutrition, health care, safety awareness, etc.

Fill in the long-term goals inventory listing some of the specific long-term goals for each area. Work from the career circle outward.

LONG-TERM GOALS INVENTORY

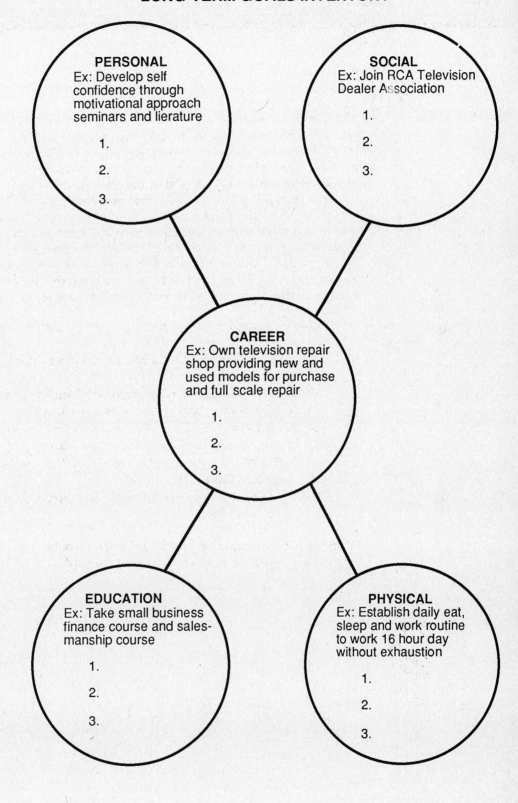

PERSONAL
Ex: Develop self
confidence through
motivational approach
seminars and lierature

1.

2.

3.

SOCIAL
Ex: Join RCA Television
Dealer Association

1.

2.

3.

CAREER
Ex: Own television repair
shop providing new and
used models for purchase
and full scale repair

1.

2.

3.

EDUCATION
Ex: Take small business
finance course and sales-
manship course

1.

2.

3.

PHYSICAL
Ex: Establish daily eat,
sleep and work routine
to work 16 hour day
without exhaustion

1.

2.

3.

SHORT-TERM GOALS: FIVE-YEAR CAREER PLAN WORK SHEET

Once you have completed the long-term inventory, take some time to reflect upon the short-term goals you want to set. Think about what you would like to be doing in your life five years from now. Then fill in the five-year career plan below.

5 YEAR CAREER PLAN

PLAN OF ACTION	JOB OBJECTIVE	JOB OBJECTIVE
	STEP 8	Get employed at reputable dealer (Speed's or Coplan's) doing full-time television repair of all models and makes.
	STEP 7	
	STEP 6	Apply to two targeted companies
	STEP 5	Read/research information about two preferred companies (Speed's/Coplan's), meet people who work there, get listing of job openings
	STEP 4	Do resume, obtain letters of recommendation, fill out applications for T.V. repair companies with openings
	STEP 3	Do informational interviewing at targeted companies
	STEP 2	Complete electronics servicing program this next fall
	STEP 1	Get part-time television repair position with local dealer

This career plan is designed like a ladder because an essential part of short-term, as well as long-term, goal setting is to determine a specific plan of action that you need to take in order to reach your goals; the plan of action you take functions like rungs on a ladder which enable you to reach the top. Without a plan of action, it is unlikely that you will reach the goals you've set.

Just as goals are more attainable when they are specific rather than general, your plan of action is easier to accomplish if it is specific. If you need some additional training to achieve your five-year career goal, it is better to write in your plan of action that you will take a course in small business ownership at the local technical school than to write "will try to learn more about owning a business."

Your plan of action should also be organized chronologically. In other words, the bottom rung of the ladder represents the first step you need to take in order to reach your goal; the second rung represents the second step in the plan, and so on up the ladder. Although the sample ladder contains eight rungs, your actual ladder may vary in length depending upon the steps needed to attain your goal.

As a final note, this career ladder concept can also be used to identify goals and plans of action for the personal, social, educational, and physical aspects of your life as well.

―――― Step 2: Choosing a Specific Occupation ―――――――――――――――――

After you have determined what career you want, it is time to nail down the specifics of the type of occupation you want. Primarily, choosing an occupation is a product of what occupational choices are available to you, what the outlook for employment in those areas is, and what places provide leads for specific jobs.

This step is going to involve considerable research on your part. Using the *occupational inventory* discussed next, identify the characteristics of an occupation that would be most suitable for you. After deciding what type of working conditions you desire, you should locate the *Dictionary of Occupational Titles* (D.O.T.) and the *Occupational Outlook Handbook* for the current year. These two resources, available in most libraries, provide information about all occupations and the possibilities for employment in each. An *occupational survey* assignment is provided next to help you identify the specific information available from these resources.

Resources available in most libraries (when read) provide valuable information when considering employment.

You also need to know where to get *job leads*. The more leads you know and use (friends, public and private agencies, want ads, etc.), the better your chances are for finding employment. Knowing about job leads is important since no one sure method works best for finding job opportunities. You will be asked to develop a list of potential job leads for the occupation of your choice.

OCCUPATIONAL INVENTORY EXERCISE

Following is a list of choices you must make before deciding on a specific occupation. Some categories offer only two choices, while other categories offer several options. Check those choices that are important to you for each category listed. As you do this, keep in mind your goals, achievements, skills, values, and interests as identified in earlier sections

1. Location

   A. _____ midwest _____ northwest _____ south _____ southwest

      _____ northeast _____ home state

   B. _____ small town _____ suburb _____ city

   C. _____ indoors _____ outdoors _____ traveling

2. Benefits

   A. _____ pay _____ security _____ prestige _____ good benefits

      _____ time off _____ flexible hours

   B. Promotions based on _____ merit _____ seniority

   C. Working hours _____ day _____ evening _____ night

3. Conditions

   A. _____ alone _____ work with others

   B. _____ small business _____ medium _____ large business

   C. _____ union _____ nonunion

   D. _____ specialist _____ varied work experiences

   E. _____ independent _____ team-led _____ manager-led

   F. _____ high pressured deadlines _____ low pressure

   G. _____ routine _____ creative

   H. _____ precision (technical) _____ rough (manual)

   I. _____ seasonal _____ constant

   J. _____ dress code _____ informal

   K. _____ responsible _____ initiative _____ non-committed

   L. _____ challenging _____ non-demanding

   M. _____ physically demanding _____ not physical

   N. _____ hazardous _____ safety assured

   O. _____ cooperation on the job _____ competition

P.   _____ influencing others   _____ instructing others

      _____ problem solving

Q.   _____ troubleshoot   _____ work on project to completion

R.   _____ frequent public contact   _____ work with tools/machines

      _____ work with information

4. Types

A.   _____ product oriented   _____ data oriented   _____ people oriented

B.   _____ industrial occupations   _____ transportation related

      _____ office occupations   _____ education related

      _____ service occupations   _____ sales

      _____ arts, design, communication   _____ agricultural

      _____ health occupations   _____ construction   _____ mechanical

      _____ scientific, technical

Occupational Survey

Preparing for a satisfying career involves more than simply learning the technical skills required for a specific occupation. Job satisfaction is also dependent upon a more comprehensive knowledge of such factors as the working conditions, opportunities for advancement, future job prospects, and so on, which encompass your occupational field of interest.

An excellent resource for discovering this type of career information is the *Occupational Outlook Handbook* published by the U.S. Department of Labor's Bureau of Labor Statistics. Your school and local community libraries should have copies of this publication.

The *Occupational Outlook Handbook* contains information about a variety of careers, grouped into six occupational areas: technicians, specialty professions, construction, mechanics and repairers, transportation and material handling, and service occupations. Within each occupational grouping, specific occupations are identified. The information provided for each occupation is listed under the following subheadings:

1. *Nature of the work*—gives a brief description of the tasks done as part of this occupation.
2. *Working conditions*—lists the kinds of circumstances under which one can expect to work.
3. *Employment*—accounts for the number of workers in the field.
4. *Training, other qualifications, and advancement*—stipulates the amount of education and related experiences necessary to enter the field, along with an indicator of advancement opportunities and procedures.
5. *Outlook*—provides general information about the number of positions available and where in the United States they can be found.
6. *Earnings*—suggests a range and average for workers who enter the field.
7. *Related occupations*—identifies occupations that are similar and might be considered.
8. *Sources of additional information*—provides the reader with a list of resources containing more information.

OCCUPATIONAL SURVEY WORK SHEET

Locate a copy of the *Occupational Outlook Handbook,* and complete the following work sheet.

State your occupation: _____

I. Nature of the Work
   A. Briefly describe the duties you are responsible for on your job.

II. Working Conditions
   A. Describe the physical setting in which you would work.

   B. Does your job involve any safety hazards? If so, what are they?

   C. How many hours per week can you expect to put in on your job?

   D. Are you required to join any type of labor organization such as a union?

   E. How many workers are currently employed in your occupation nationwide?

   F. In what particular areas of the country are job opportunities in your field most likely to be found?

III. Required Qualifications

A. What kind of educational background are you required to have?

B. What specific kinds of technical skills must you acquire for the job?

C. Identify any on-the-job training that will be needed.

IV. Employment Outlook

A. What rate of future employment is expected in your occupation?

V. Earnings and Benefits

A. What is the average hourly and/or annual starting salary?

B. What kinds of salary increases might you expect?

C. What are the possibilities for promotion or advancement on the job?

D. What fringe benefits are part of the job? (ie., health and life insurance, sick leave, paid vacations, etc.)

VI. Related Occupations

    A. List several occupations that are closely related to your occupation.

VII. Trade Publications

    A. List the title of two trade publications that could supply you with additional occupational information.

Finding Job Leads

Now that you know, or at least have some idea of what you want from employment, the next logical question is how do you get the job that is right for you?

Finding the right job, or a good job in today's economy, challenges the most talented and skilled worker. The strategies you employ in your job search may be as varied as the shopping techniques you use to buy a car.

Suppose you were buying a car, and you knew just what style and options you wanted. You would probably start looking for leads by checking the newspaper ads, visiting dealers, reading auto shoppers' catalogs, and asking friends and family. You may know from experience that all of these leads can be productive, some more than others.

One placement specialist advises that the chance of finding a job increases as the number of job leads increases. Others suggest that you zero in on one job and develop leads which will result in getting that job. Still others believe that your best chances come from the backdoor approach of "interviewing for information" to tap the hidden job market. Regardless of which method you choose, job leads are essential for finding the right place of employment to put your skills to work.

Six Types of Job Leads

Six basic types of leads should be considered when looking for your ideal job: personal contacts, school placement services, private agencies, classified ads, trade journals, and the hidden job market. Let's look at each in turn.

Personal contacts are by far your best source of productive job leads. The importance of these contacts lies in the fact that employers prefer to hire someone who is known rather than take a chance on a stranger. Even if you know someone who knows someone who knows someone else, you're still regarded as an acquaintance. The people you especially want to become acquainted with are workers in the area of your desired occupation. This preference for hiring friends and those known to other workers is one major reason why 80 percent of jobs are never advertised. This lends credibility to the statement, "It's not what you know, but who you know."

How do you tap into the system of people who are known in the industry? One of the most effective ways is through your family and friends. Another is through churches, clubs, organizations, or groups to which you belong. The places where you spend your time and money may also be sources of job leads.

Let it be known to as many people as possible, to anyone and everyone, that you want to work at a specific job. If you obtain any leads from these people, follow up on the leads immediately. Make contact with the prospective employer even if the job isn't exactly what you're looking for; it may be the link to the job you are looking for. Often those who are hiring know others who are also hiring.

Take time out of your active life to tell folks about yourself: your career plans, your abilities, and your need for a job. Emphasize your training and skills. Be positive and enthusiastic about work. Emphasize your desire for a full-time job and settling down. Sound serious about applying your skills and learning more.

You can't sit back and expect to tap into this system. Family and friends won't go looking for jobs for you, but they will help if you make your needs known. By talking with these people, you'll have a chance to find out more about yourself and your field while practicing your interviewing skills.

No guarantee exists that this or any other system will land you a job, but by using these contacts, you become assertive. You look interested and eager; family and friends will continue to promote you when they see the effort you're putting forth.

Another source of leads is the school placement office, which provides excellent contacts for many graduates. Placement counselors, who know the program offerings of your school, are also familiar with the employment needs of local business and industry who hire graduates. In addition, many placement departments provide services such as job boards, graduate referrals, mailing lists, résumé writing and typing, campus interviews, and specialized career counseling. Stop at your school placement office, find out what services they offer, and register for those you need.

A third source, private agencies, help secure employment for a price. Many are specialized for particular occupational areas. Some require payment from the applicant, some from the employer, and some collect from both. Most require a contract of some sort. Fees may range from 50 to 120 percent of your first month's earnings. Agencies are worth contacting to see what jobs are available. You'll find the yellow pages helpful for the names, addresses, and phone numbers of agencies in your area.

Another source to consider is that old standby, the Sunday paper. The ads are neatly classified for all to see; some employers use this source exclusively. If the statistics are accurate, however, only 20 percent of available jobs are listed in the want ads. But don't dismiss ads; your job may be there. The secret to using the classified ads is in knowing how to read them.

Essentially three kinds of ads appear in the paper: open, blind, and spot. Open ads provide the most information about the position. They identify the firm, the position, even wage range. You respond directly to the person identified in the ad.

Blind ads provide limited information about the job or list only the position and the requirements. They ask the applicant to respond to a box number or the newspaper. This technique helps the employer screen applicants and discourage the casual job seeker. Employers place blind ads in newspapers, at times, to survey the potential work force in a given occupation. The employer may not even have a position available. Remember, employers take a box number and use blind ads so they don't have to respond to applicants.

Employment agencies place spot ads to promote positions they have listed and to develop a list of potential workers to place in the future. These ads may offer several positions and wage ranges, but such ads do not identify the employer.

When you use the classified ads, read them faithfully; respond immediately to new ads. Be prepared to send a résumé and letter of application quickly in response to new ads.

Don't overlook another source, trade journals, which offer specialized job opportunities for technicians and professionals. Firms usually seek experienced people among the ranks of those active in a specific field. Both open and blind ads appear in these journals. Respond to these ads as you would those in the newspaper.

Finally, the "hidden job market,"[8] which Richard Irish writes about in his book *Go Hire Yourself an Employer*, becomes available to the applicant who seeks leads by interviewing for information.

Applicants, particularly students, make contacts with those actively employed in their chosen field, question these professionals, and discuss the future

---

[8]Irish, op. cit. pp. 79–85.

of the occupation. Irish suggests that applicants approach employers and supervisors in their field, not to seek employment but to seek information.

Prior to graduation, students can conduct a series of interviews with professionals to obtain a realistic view of their occupation and, more importantly, to make contacts for later when they will be seeking employment. These interviews involve asking a series of questions ranging from "How did you get started in this business?" to "What changes do you see occurring in this field in the next ten years?" Any of these leads may result in employment; all have worked for applicants in the past. Try not to limit yourself to only one source of job leads. Be persistent and optimistic about finding new leads and a new job.

JOB LEADS WORK SHEET

Complete the following assignment.

1. List three people that you know in your chosen occupation.

2. Go to your school placement office. What services do they provide? How do you apply for these services?

3. Name three employment agencies in your local area that you would consider contacting for employment help.

4. Out of the Sunday newspaper, cut out an example of each of the following three employment advertisements: open, blind, and spot.

5. List two trade journals for your field. Give examples of two types of jobs listed in the employment section of those journals.

6. Name three companies that you would really like to work for. Then list five questions you might ask if you were interviewing them for information.

   Three company names

   Five questions you might ask

_____ Step 3: Getting Employed _____

This third step in the employment process is perhaps the most crucial. Basically, this step involves preparing yourself to be interviewed. It is during the interview that you get to "sell" yourself to an employer.

The steps involved in securing employment are as follows:

1. Gathering data through a *personal inventory*. This includes your employment history, educational history, references, personal history, and military history (if applicable).

2. Putting together a *résumé*. This short, one- or two-page summary presents your most desirable qualities: personal, educational, and experiential.

3. Writing *letters of application*. This cover letter, sent along with the résumé, introduces you, highlights your qualifications, and requests an interview.

4. Filling out *application forms*. The key to success in this area is to be neat, complete, and honest.

5. *Interviewing* for a position. Many people are eliminated before even reaching this stage. So if given an interview, you'll need to present yourself, both verbally and nonverbally, in a way that highlights your desirable qualities.

6. Writing *follow-up letters*. This final contact reminds the interviewer that you're interested in and qualified for the position.

One way to view the job seeking process is as an advertising campaign. First, a campaign program consists of having a salable product (your qualifications), and second, of making frequent contact with the consumer (the employer), *without being a pest!* Notice how five of the six steps in this employment process involve "making contact."

Let us now examine the above six steps in securing employment in depth.

Gathering Personal Information

As you begin your personal job search, you will succeed by using the strategy of an advertising campaign. Your technical expertise and social skills represent the product you are trying to "sell" to an employer in a job market that is often highly competitive. The promotional techniques you will use to market these skills include the résumé, letter of application, application forms, the interview, and follow-up letters. You close the deal and sell yourself when the employer offers you the job.

Although there are many and varied techniques for marketing your skills, a combination of the following information is generally highlighted:

1. *Personal Data*—name, address, phone number, date of birth, height, weight, condition of health, marital status, and military service status.
2. *Education*—technical schools, colleges, specialized training, and high schools. Highlight major courses taken, degrees earned, academic honors, and extracurricular activities.
3. *Employment Experience*—names, addresses, and phone numbers of current and former employers. List a brief description of the duties and responsibilities for each job listed.
4. *Additional Qualifications*—Hobbies, interests, memberships in social or service organizations, honors and awards.
5. *References*—Names, titles, addresses and phone numbers of competent individuals who are able to provide employers with an assessment of your technical skills, character, work record, or education.

Now that you are aware of the kinds of information commonly asked for during the employment process, you may want to take some time to think about this information and compile a list of your own qualifications.

The most challenging step you are faced with is presenting your qualifications in a clear, meaningful, and interesting way that represents your uniqueness as a prospective employee. Pulling together pertinent information from your experiences can seem overwhelming; this task can be simplified considerably if you are well organized.

A tool that can assist you in organizing this information is the "personal qualifications inventory"—in which you list your job-related qualifications. This list will provide a foundation from which you can draw information to be incorporated into every contact with your prospective employer.

PERSONAL QUALIFICATIONS INVENTORY WORK SHEET

In the following space provided, list your qualifications for the position you are seeking. Consider your skills and achievements, your education and training, and your work record and experience as the basis for these qualifications. Examples of what to include on your list are as follows:

1. Completed secretarial diploma program.
2. Experienced using all forms of word processing.
3. Outstanding work record with present employer; have not missed a day of work in two years.

1. Will complete an Associate of Arts Degree In May 1991.

2. Achieved a 4.0 In College. Maintained a 3.9.

3. Competed in English Scholarship Team in 9th grade — won honorable mention.

4. Have skills in special events planning and budgeting.

5. Great work records — always on time.

6. Great performance of duties — won employee of month twice.

7. Communication skills. Dealt with customers, supervisors, & peers on a professional level.

8.

9.

10.

Résumés

After you've completed the "Personal Qualifications Inventory," you are ready to organize and develop your own personal résumé. Many different styles of résumés are appropriate; you must simply choose the style that you feel most comfortable with and that you believe presents your qualifications to the greatest advantage.

Résumés can be categorized as "living" or "dead." A living résumé contains vivid personal descriptions of your experiences and abilities in brief sentence form; it makes you "come to life" on the printed page. A "dead" résumé, on the other hand, merely lists facts about your background and is far less interesting and personal for an employer to read.

On the following pages, you will find examples of various résumés upon which you may pattern your own. You may find the suggestions below helpful when creating your own résumé:

1. Don't "date" your résumé by including today's date in the heading or your age in the Personal Data section. For example, it is better to list "Date of Birth" rather than current age since the former remains constant.

2. Immediately following the heading, include a Career or Employment Objective which identifies the positions you are applying for and reflects your long- and short-term goals.

3. Beneath the Employment Objective, place your Education of Work Experience depending upon which of the two you want to emphasize first for an employer.

4. Write short descriptions, using active verbs to clarify the skills and experiences you've identified in the Work and Education sections. Your education and work experiences should be listed with the most recent first.

For every job must have job description

5. Provide additional information about "who you are" by listing honors you've received and professional organizations to which you belong.

6. Include any personal data, such as height, weight, date of birth, etc., which you believe would enhance your desirability as an employee.

7. Obtain three references. Generally choose two people who can discuss your technical skills and abilities and one person to serve as a character reference. It's a good idea if your references represent individuals with varied backgrounds, such as a clergyman, teacher, and former employer. These references should not be related to you.

8. Contact persons you want to use as references in order to obtain their permission. Not only is this a matter of common courtesy, but it also prepares your references for phone calls and/or letters from employers seeking information about you. Sometimes job seekers choose not to list references on the résumé; they prefer to indicate that such references will be provided to the employer "upon request."

(in margins around — prefer more)

9. Keep your résumé one to two pages. Busy employers or personnel managers may be unwilling to read résumés that are longer. If your résumé runs longer than one page, it should be continued on a second page rather than on the back side of the first page. Include an appropriate heading in the top left-hand corner of the second page: For example, "Resume of Sandy Smith—Page Two."

10. Proofread your neatly typed résumé for spelling and typographical errors. Consider having your résumé typeset by a printer. It's relatively inexpensive and looks professional.

11. Make your résumé as visually appealing and easy to read as possible. Balance the printed material with sufficient white space. Use underlining, capitalization, and boldface type or italics to make important information stand out.
12. Use a good quality, heavy bond paper, of white or off-white. Avoid pastels or other unusual colored paper, as well as tissue thin, erasable typing paper.
13. Duplicate quality copies of your résumé. Find a print shop that can make professional copies rather than using the copy machine found in your local library. Professional duplication may cost you a few cents more per copy, but you can select the quality of paper you want for your copies.

6 major categories for Résumé

Job Objective
Qualifications (skills)
Experience
Education
References – not on résumé
Affiliations / Honors

Do résumé one

SAMPLE RÉSUMÉS

TERRY ARAGON
3976 ELMBROOK COURT
MUNCIE, ARKANSAS 98654
(319) 871-0548

EMPLOYMENT OBJECTIVE:	**Appliance Service Repair**

ACADEMIC HISTORY:

1989–1990	**Pleasant Valley Technical College** 8234 Madison Avenue Pleasant Valley, Arkansas 98965
Program:	**Appliance Servicing:** (One-year vocational diploma program), entered to develop skills in appliance field. Courses taken included Appliance Servicing (two semesters), Appliance Electronics, Industrial Communication, Applied Psychology, and Industrial Mathematics (one semester each). Placed on Dean's Honor List.

EMPLOYMENT HISTORY:

1988 to present	**Pleasant Valley Technical College** 8234 Madison Avenue Pleasant Valley, Arkansas 98965 (319) 691-8765
	Laboratory Assistant: Helped students set up projects in Commercial Refrigeration and Heating classes. Demonstrated proper use of test instruments and gauges. Selected proper tools for students.
1984–1988	**Little Rock Metro Transit** P.O. Box 94 Little Rock, Arkansas 98756 (319) 987-6543
	Coach Operator: Transported passengers over specified routes to local points according to time schedule. Collected cash fares from passengers. Regulated heating, lighting, and ventilating systems for passenger comfort. Complied with local traffic regulations.

Terry Aragon–page 2

Road Supervisor: Supervised drivers and coordinated bus schedules to maintain service. Instructed drivers in operation of various types of buses. Observed and recorded number of passengers on buses. Adjusted complaints of passengers regarding service.

SPECIAL ACHIEVEMENTS:

Diploma in Appliance Service; Member Refrigeration Service Engineers Society; Political Campaign Chairman; Chauffeur's License.

SPECIAL SKILLS:

Prompt, reliable, hard worker, take pride in my work, work well with others, willing to learn, and will work overtime.

REFERENCES:

Gladly furnished upon request.

LEE BURNS
9876 HARTLAND STREET
TROY, CONNECTICUT 17581
(606) 768-9453

EMPLOYMENT OBJECTIVE: Automotive Servicing Technician

EDUCATION:

January 1988 to present   Southwest County Technical Institute
                                       Redding, Connecticut 17596

                                       Currently enrolled in the Automotive Servicing
                                       Program; anticipate completion with certificate May
                                       1989.

EMPLOYMENT HISTORY:

February 1985 to present   Golden Dairy Co-op Troy, Connecticut

                                       Operate one-gallon plastic bottle producing
                                       machinery; inspect and adjust equipment for
                                       uniform efficiency; serve customers directly; write
                                       sales receipts; operate forklift; unload tankers of raw
                                       milk; set up orders of products for distribution to
                                       stores.

January 1981 to February 1985   U.S. Navy USS Wisconsin (LSD–30)
                                       Atlantic Post Office, New York, New York.

                                       Monitored closed circuit television equipment;
                                       prepared daily news broadcasts; coordinated weekly
                                       program scheduling; spliced and repaired movie
                                       film.

PART-TIME EMPLOYMENT: Insulated houses; delivered construction materials;
                                       inventoried electric heat and air conditioning
                                       products; set up orders; worked on farm; child care
                                       worker supervising emotionally disturbed children;
                                       mowed lawns; painted houses; reconditioned
                                       fiberglass boats.

ACTIVITIES: Leather craft, camping, fishing, bowling, lap
                                       swimming, and hiking.

REFERENCES: Gladly furnished upon request.

TONY ROBERTS
2962 ROOSEVELT AVENUE
LA JOLLA, CALIFORNIA 97585
(213) 759-3948

CAREER OBJECTIVE: Account Clerk in modern financial office with
                                      opportunity for advancement.

EMPLOYMENT: Hometown Pharmacy
                                      Alameda, California

                                      Office Manager—March 1988 to present

                                      Assist in billing and accounts receivable. Calculate
                                      inventory, verify invoices, authorize purchases of
                                      various items, handle cash, monitor store operations,
                                      process insurance forms, chart and file patient cards.
                                      Excellent communication and telephone skills.

                                      Modern Interiors, Incorporated
                                      La Jolla, California

                                      Clerical Assistant—February 1985 to February 1988

                                      Responsible for bookkeeping, accounts
                                      receivable/payable, and tax statements.

EDUCATION: Riverview Business College
                                      Riverview, California

                                      Diploma: Account Clerk
                                      Graduate: May 1989
                                      Grade Point Average: 3.8/4.0

                                      Courses studied: Bookkeeping I-II, Typing I-II (speed
                                      45-50 wpm), Business Math, Calculating Machines,
                                      Data Entry Techniques, Filing and Communication
                                      I-II.

AWARDS AND ACHIEVEMENTS: President's Honor List, RBC, 1988-89
                                      Outstanding Business Student, 1989
                                      Class Treasurer, 1989
                                      Perfect Attendance Award

REFERENCES: Excellent references provided on request.

RÉSUMÉ WORK SHEET AND ASSIGNMENT

Read through the following work sheet, collect the information needed to complete the assignment, and fill in the blanks. Be as complete as possible. Do not use any abbreviations. Be sure to use as many action words as possible when describing job duties (see Life Skills worksheet p. 136).

When finished, organize the information into a working résumé that includes each category on the work sheet and highlights the qualifications that relate to your professional objective. Follow the previously mentioned guidelines for creating effective résumés.

_____

(Full Name)

_____

(Street Address)

_____

(City, State, and Zip)

_____

(Area Code and Telephone Number)

EMPLOYMENT OBJECTIVE: _____

_____

EDUCATION:

_____   _____

(Graduated or Dates Attended)   *(Name of Most Recent School)*

_____

(City and State)

Program: _____

(List Degree, Major Courses, Acquired Skills,

_____

and Grade Point Average in this Section)

_____

_____

_____   _____
(Graduated or Dates Attended)   (Name of Most Recent School)

                                                   _____
                                                          (City and State)

Program: _____
                                            (List Degree, Major Courses, Acquired Skills,

                                                   _____
                                             and Grade Point Average in this Section)

                                                   _____

                                                   _____

                                                   _____

WORK EXPERIENCE:

_____   _____
       (Dates Employed)   (Name of Most Recent Company)

                                                   _____
                                                          (Street Address)

                                                   _____
                                                      (City, State, and Zip)

                                                   _____
                                                 (Area Code and Telephone Number)

                                                   _____
                                                          (Job Title)

                                                   _____
                                                    (List Specific Job Duties)

                                                   _____

                                                   _____

Reader: Repeat the above format as many times as necessary to list all previous employers and work experience.

HONORS AND AWARDS
SCHOOL AND COMMUNITY
ACTIVITIES:

_____

_____

_____

_____

PROFESSIONAL AFFILIATIONS:

_____

_____

_____

_____

PERSONAL DATA:

_____

(May include Place of Birth, Date of Birth, Height, Weight, Health Condition,

_____

Military Status, Hobbies, Interests, etc.)

_____

_____

REFERENCES:

_____
(Name)

_____
(Position)

_____
(Company)

_____
(Address)

_____
(City, State, and Zip)

_____
(Area Code and Telephone Number)

Note: List at least three references using the above format.

Letter of Application

Applicants who send résumés to prospective employers need a cover letter to accompany their résumés. These letters of application also provide an excellent opportunity for applicants to sell themselves by emphasizing qualifications and personality traits.

The letter of application is often the employer's first contact with the applicant; it provides a first impression which can make or break the chances for employment. As the first piece of work presented to the employer, this letter must be well written and effective.

Typed in a standard business letter format, the letter of application includes the following parts: the heading (your return address and the date); the inside address (the name and mailing address of the employer); the greeting (a formal acknowledgement of your reader); the body (three or four paragraphs that are described in detail next); the complimentary closing (a traditional ending for the letter); and finally your signature.

The three paragraphs of the body are the most important part of the letter of application. The first paragraph identifies the specific position applied for and the source of the job lead. The second presents the primary qualifications for the position, and the final paragraph requests an interview. Each element will be discussed in turn.

Beginning the letter may be the most challenging part of writing it. Several stock introductions may be employed. Typically the letter should name the source of the job lead (the placement office, an instructor, a newspaper ad), identify the specific job applied for, and express interest in the position.

The second paragraph in the body of the letter of application ought to answer the question, "Why should you be hired for this specific job?" The best way to answer this question is to present your strongest qualifications for the position. Relevant work experience and/or education could be mentioned. Each may be developed in a separate paragraph.

Discuss specific skills, concepts and procedures, equipment and machines, and abilities and talents that have been learned on other jobs or in your training. Be specific; use proper names and technical language to show the employer that you have valid qualifications for this position. Generally, students don't supply enough specific information about their abilities in these paragraphs. You can alert the employer to additional information that appears on your enclosed résumé.

Think of the salesperson who is showing you a used car. What happens if the only thing you are told is, "It's a good runner"? Are you convinced? Contrast that to the seller who talks about the mileage, the condition of the exhaust system, the sound of the engine, the quality of the tires, the recent paint job, etc. In the same way details sell products, they also sell people. Be sure to include enough specific details about yourself in the body of the letter.

The final paragraph of the letter of application requests an interview to discuss your qualifications for the position. Make yourself available at the employer's convenience, and state how and when you can be contacted.

None of the paragraphs in the body needs to be long; three to five sentences will do. They should be typed, well written, and accurate in both spelling and punctuation. Use the form of a standard business letter, be clear, and above all, be neat.

SAMPLE LETTERS OF APPLICATION

Review the sample letters of application that are provided on the following pages. Evaluate each using the guidelines just discussed. Put yourself in the shoes of the employer, and ask yourself if this letter comes from a person you would like to talk to about a job. Finally, take one of the open or blind advertisements that you collected for your "job leads" assignment, and type an effective letter of application which will make an employer say, "This is the person we've been looking for!"

SAMPLE 1
1234 Main Street
Hometown, Minnesota 51234
April 10, 1989

Block
— need this when mailing
it in.

Mr. Joseph Smith, Manager
Acme Autoland
567 North State Avenue
St. Paul, Minnesota 59876

Dear Mr. Smith:

I am writing in response to your advertisement for an auto body repairman in the Sunday, April 5, 1989, edition of *The St. Paul Pioneer Press.* Please accept this letter as my application for this position.

I am presently enrolled in the Auto Body Program at Waukesha County Technical Institute. In this program, I have learned skills in rust repair, panel replacement and alignment, metal finishing, leading, frame straightening, painting, and unibody construction and repair.

I am also enrolled in related courses consisting of auto body welding, industrial math, communication, psychology, auto schematics, and auto body estimating. The training I'm receiving in these classes will enhance my ability to be a productive worker for your business.

Due to my interest in this field, I have in the past restored two collector's cars to showroom condition. I have been employed in the past at Joe's Service Station where I have learned the skills needed to restore these two vehicles. My enclosed résumé presents greater detail about my previous job experience.

I would greatly appreciate an interview with you at your convenience. I can be reached at (207) 789-5432 after 3:00 p.m., should you have any questions.

Sincerely,

Jan Richards

Enclosure: Résumé

SAMPLE 2
1684 West Colfax Avenue
Denver, Colorado 80267
May 23, 1989

Ms. Jean Wexler
Director of Personnel
Lance Manufacturing Company
309 Clyde Gallager Road
Arvada, Colorado 80003

Dear Ms. Wexler:

I wish to be considered as an applicant for the payroll clerk position advertised in *The Rocky Mountain News* on May 21, 1989.

On May 12, 1989, I graduated from Red Rocks Community College with a Diploma in Accounting Services. I have been thoroughly trained in payroll procedures throughout my education and have received hands-on experience as well. Currently I am employed at Casa Bonita as a Swing Manager, and part of my responsibilities include auditing time cards and preparing payroll. I am also employed at the Aurora City Hall Treasurer's Office where I work with taxes and interest computation.

I feel this position would be just what I am searching for, and I am confident that I would be an asset to your company. Please feel free to contact me at your convenience. I may be reached at 637-4932 between 4-10 p.m. Monday through Friday.

Sincerely,

Chris Powell

Enclosure: Résumé

Application Forms

Unless you have sent a letter of application and résumé, the application form is likely to be the first written work that you turn in to an employer. As such, applications are a representation of you and the quality of your work. Applications not only reveal your education and experience but show whether you can write without error, follow directions, and express yourself clearly and understandably. It is also important to see the application as an official document expressing your desire for employment and to realize that it becomes part of your official employment file. Therefore, be sure to fill out the application in pen.

Read through the entire application form before filling in any information. Take a careful look at the layout and types of questions the application contains. These few minutes spent previewing the form will prevent unnecessary errors later.

Generally, the applications that make the grade for employers meet three criteria. Accuracy and honesty are first. Employment officers believe that if you lie on an application, you would also lie (and cheat, rob, and murder) on the job. Honesty is so important that nearly all applications have a disclaimer that allows the company to terminate your employment whenever dishonesty is discovered.

Second, applications should be complete. Applications are only helpful to an employer when they contain the information that employers are asking for. Some questions on the form may not pertain to you, such as military status (if you've never been in the service) or number of dependents (if you have none). Still, the employer wants to know that you saw the question. For those items that do not apply or those for which you don't have an answer, respond with N/A (not applicable) or a slash like — or /.

Finally, the third standard for judging an application is clarity and neatness. For that reason, it is always best to print your answers (except where your legal signature is required at the bottom of the application). Take your time when filling out the application, and correct errors with a single slash through the error with the correction on the side.

An application is divided into several sections including personal information, position desired, education, employment experience, military service, references, health record, and legal signature. Some of the following suggestions may be helpful to you when filling out an application blank.

1. Salary—write "open" or "negotiable," or give a range (for example, $22,000 to 25,000) or state a figure based on research that you've done.

2. Reason for leaving—be honest; if fired from a previous job, write "terminated" or "will explain during interview" with the hope of having the opportunity to explain your situation.

3. Criminal record—if you were ever convicted of a felony, be honest and hope to explain how you've reformed. This question does not apply to "minor" traffic violations or misdemeanors.

4. Position desired—list the specific job for which you are applying (clerk, typist, travel agent, electronics technician, maintenance mechanic, etc.) avoid "anything available" answers.

5. Fine print—be sure to read the fine print above the place for your signature and the day's date. Employers sometimes ask for authorization an extensive search into your past and present.

6. Signature—don't forget to sign the application form; your signature veri-
   fies that all of your information is correct to the best of your knowledge.

Finally, keep in mind that the more flexible you appear on an application, the more attractive you will apper to an employer. This flexibility will be
revealed in your willingness to work alternate shifts, be open to salary negoti-
ation, be willing to travel, etc.

Job Interviews

Regardless of unemployment and economic conditions, one to two million jobs are filled every year. Even under the most difficult economic times, you can still find a job, but the number of people you will be competing against is greatly increased. Nevertheless, whether you are competing against 10 or 100 individuals, the interview is by far the most important step in the selection process. In the interview, the employer will decide which of the qualified applicants will be hired.

Taken from an interviewer's perspective, your ticket to getting a job is being the most desirable candidate in the field of applicants. Interviewers are trying to match qualified applicants with the company's work needs. They try to recognize potential leaders for their company. They seek people they "like" and trust. Interviewers want to feel that they know you and know what to expect from you. The interview provides you with an opportunity to show employers that you are "their kind of person."

The job interview process consists of three stages. The first step involves preparing for the interview. The second step is the actual interview itself. The final step involves follow-up activities after the interview.

Preparing for the interview. Preparing for an interview is essential if success is to be attained and employment gained. Most of the information gathering to prepare yourself for an interview has been dealt with thus far: knowing your goals, values, interests, achievements, and skills; knowing the outlook and characteristics of your chosen profession; writing résumés and letters of application; and filling out job applications. It would be helpful to review these steps before the interview to remind you of what you have to offer an employer.

Preparing for the interview also requires gathering information about the company. Know the products and services the company provides, its customers and competitors, and its history and recent successes. This information can be found through a variety of sources. Check your local library for various business and manufacturing directories. Review the company's quarterly or yearly report. Talk to current employees, former employees, or others with knowledge of the company. Find out as much as you can about the specific job. The information you gather in this way will also allow you to carry on a well-informed conversation with the employer and show your interest in the company.

It is also valuable to begin to develop a professional attitude by knowing the latest trends in your field of expertise. Trade journals are a potential source of this information. Employers want to know that you are interested in their company and that you desire to be the best in your chosen field.

The next step in preparing for the real interview involves doing mock interviews. This practice helps you to develop confidence and skill in talking about your qualifications. In addition, such rehearsals enable you to anticipate difficult questions and save you from becoming flustered by unexpected questions.

Knowing the location of the interview and the length of time it takes to get there is also important. It is essential that you arrive between five to ten minutes before the interview. Arriving late is one way to guarantee you won't be hired. A test run to assure direction and timing may be required if you are unfamiliar with the location. If for some reason you must arrive late, call the interviewer immediately, explain the circumstances, and suggest an alternative meeting time.

Equally important is dressing appropriately for the interview. The key is to look neat, clean, and conservative. Don't dress in flashy colors or wear faded or soiled blue jeans. The key word is appropriate! Dress as you feel the interviewer will be dressed.

Interviewing techniques.   Entering the company building begins the next stage in the interview process. Be courteous and polite to all the people you come in contact with. Interviewers will often ask others what they thought of you (secretaries, office mates, etc.). If you are rude and disrespectful to others, the message usually will reach the interviewer. Knowing the interviewer's name and using it also shows positive interpersonal skills.

Research suggests that an interviewer decides to hire you or not in the first few minutes of the interview. Being on time, dressing appropriately, and being friendly and pleasant during the first contact with an interviewer are most important.

When called into the interviewer's office, let the interviewer take the lead. If a hand is extended to you, extend yours. If you are asked to be seated, do so. Wait to see which direction the interview goes. The interviewer may engage you in small talk or may provide you with valuable information about the company. Regardless of how the meeting proceeds, listen and respond accordingly.

During the interview, you will be asked a variety of questions. Respond with honesty and completeness, reflecting your positive attitude. Make sure your answers are truthful and accurate since dishonesty is a major reason for rejecting applicants. Don't give one or two word answers. Explain what you mean, and give concrete examples as proof. Interviewers dislike having to force information out of you. Answer the question directly. If you are unsure of what the interviewer is asking, paraphrase the question to clarify any misunderstanding.

In all of your answers, emphasize the positive. Even if an employer asks questions about your weaknesses, respond positively. For example, to the question, "What are your work-related weaknesses?" respond with a negative that is really a positive such as "I work too hard" or "I'm a perfectionist." If you do share a weakness, such as "I was late to my last job too many times," suggest how you've corrected the error such as, "but now I have a reliable car that I won't have trouble starting in the morning."

Your nonverbal communication conveys much in the interview process. You will need to show that you are confident (but not cocky), energetic, and enthusiastic about the prospects of employment. Don't smoke or chew gum, even if offered to you. Sit up in your chair and lean slightly forward. Try not to cross your arms or legs. Make eye contact. Smile. Say "please" and "thank-you" when appropriate.

Throughout the interview, you will want to stress your ability to get along with others, your assertiveness, your honesty, your open-mindedness, your flexibility, and your creativity and other personal qualities you have. This can be accomplished by offering examples from your personal and work-related achievements.

At the close of the interview, employers will give you a chance to ask questions. Use this opportunity to show interest in the company, and listen to the answers that you get. Prior research you did on the company will allow you to ask relevant and appropriate questions such as, "In what direction do you think the company is heading during the next five to ten years?" or "What recent innovations have affected the electronics department here?" Avoid questions about salary, vacation time, sick days, etc. These are important questions that should be asked only after being offered the job.

End the interview on a positive note. Take time to make your final pitch. Look the interviewer in the eye, express your sincere interest in the job, and reinforce your strongest qualifications for the position. You will want the interviewer to remember you and your qualifications. Let the interviewer conclude the interview, express thanks for the time and attention, and find out when a decision will be made and how you will be contacted.

Immediately after the interview, write a follow-up "thank you" letter. If you don't hear from the interviewer when indicated, call and ask if a decision has been made.

Why Applicants are Rejected

In addition to knowing the essential techniques for successful interviewing, you should also be aware of the reasons that applicants are rejected in interviews. Research done at Northwestern University identified common reasons for not hiring a candidate.[9] The most frequent reasons for rejection follow:

1. Poor personal appearance.
2. Being close-minded, aggressive, and conceited.
3. Inability to express oneself clearly.
4. Lack of knowledge of career and personal goals; indecisive.
5. Lack of interest and enthusiasm.
6. Lack of confidence, poise, and tact.
7. Failure to participate in activities in the past.
8. Too interested in "give-me's" (money, etc.).
9. Poor grades.
10. Reluctance to change.

Other reasons for rejection include criticizing former employers and co-workers, failure to make eye contact, sloppy application, lack of knowledge in field of specialization, low moral standards, strong prejudices, and being late to the interview without reason.

In short, the best interview is one that requires considerable planning, presenting yourself positively throughout the interview, and making contact one final time through follow-up letters to remind the employer of your desire to work. Remember, employers are looking for reasons to hire you. Give them good reason to!

[9]Frank S. Endicott, "Making the Most of Your Job Interview," A New York Life Insurance Company Pamphlet. © by the Placement Center, Northwestern University, Evanston, IL.

JOB INTERVIEW ASSIGNMENT

Pair up with another person. Ask the person a minimum of seven questions and a maximum of ten questions form the "55 Most Frequently Asked Questions"[10] sheet that immediately follows, then fill out the evaluation sheet.

Most Frequently Asked Questions During Job Interviews

1. Why do you want to work for our company?
2. Tell me something about your last job.
3. How do you feel about your last employer?
4. Why did you leave your last job?
5. Do you feel that you are mature enough to handle the responsibilities of this job?
6. What salary do you expect to be getting here?
7. What are your future career plans?
8. How do you spend your spare time?
9. Are you taking any courses right now?
10. Tell me something about yourself.
11. At school, what courses did you like best? Least? Why?
12. What one person had the greatest influence on your life and why?
13. Why did you choose this particular field of work?
14. How did you finance your way through school?
15. How did you rate scholastically in your senior year in high school?
16. Where do you hope to be five years from now? Ten years from now? What is your ultimate professional goal?
17. What prompted you to apply for our company?
18. How does your family feel about your career choice and its requirements?
19. What, in your estimation, is the key to professional success, particularly in this job?
20. Are you looking for temporary or permanent work?
21. What is your concept of the ideal boss?
22. Do you have friends or relatives working for our company?
23. Have you ever been in trouble with the law? Explain.
24. Are you free to travel? Relocate? Any restrictions?
25. What, in your opinion, especially qualifies you for this job? Explain fully.
26. What books, magazines, or newspapers do you read regularly?
27. Have you ever been fired from a job? If so, why? Explain fully.
28. Are you in a position to work overtime when necessary?
29. What is your draft status? Are you registered? Do you have plans for the military?
30. Do you suffer from any allergies or recurring illnesses?
31. How far did you go with your formal education? Why did you stop at that point?
32. Is this a field of work you'll want to stay in? Explain why.

[10] *Ibid.*

33. How is your memory for names and faces? Fine details?

34. How would you describe yourself as an employee?

35. Do you belong to any professional organizations related to this job? Are you willing to join such organizations?

36. What do you know about our product line and services? Explain fully.

37. Who are our competitors in this field? Explain how their product lines and services compete with ours.

38. Have you ever supervised people? Ever trained someone on the job? If so, how many?

39. What, in your opinion, is the value of your vocational education?

40. What foreign languages do you speak? Would you feel comfortable around people who speak a language other than your own?

41. How long would it take you to get to and from work? What kind of car do you have? Is it reliable? Are you punctual and reliable?

42. How will automation affect the future of our industry and your job? How are you preparing for this change?

43. How would you react to working under the supervision of a younger person?

44. What sports do you excel in? What do you get out of those sports?

45. What in your estimation is the outstanding achievement in your life?

46. What are your pet peeves?

47. Is it all right to call your previous employer for a reference? What do you think he'll tell me?

48. Do you picture yourself being promoted quickly in this company?

49. Have the people you've worked with ever made any difference to you on a job?

50. Have you ever applied here before? When? Did you follow up on the application? Why or why not?

51. Would you want your salary increases to be based on merit, promotional examination, or length of commitment?

52. Would you object to a training or probationary period when we hire you?

53. Tell me what one outstanding quality should make me hire you rather than one of the other people applying for this job.

54. What is your best work quality?

55. What would you do if you found a co-worker taking home company tools against company policy?

Evaluation Sheet

Write the number of the question you have asked. Try to remember the "essence" of your partner's responses. You may want to jot down answers that you thought were especially good or those that could be improved. We will use these answers for discussion. Throughout the interview, rate the applicant using the Interview Rating Scale.

1. Question # _____
   Answer:

2. Question # _____

Answer:

3. Question # _____

Answer:

4. Question # _____

Answer:

5. Question # _____

Answer:

6. Question # _____

Answer:

7. Question # _____

Answer:

8. Question # _____

Answer:

9. Question # _____

Answer:

10. Question # _____

Answer:

Interview Rating Scale

Applicant: _____   Interviewer: _____

Rate on a scale of 1–4 the applicant's overall skills in the areas listed next. Use the following scale:

    4 = Excellent
    3 = Good
    2 = Fair
    1 = Needs work

Verbal Skills

_____   1. Honest, sincere, and consistent answers

_____   2. Openness: volunteers information and provides examples

_____   3. Answers questions directly; non-evasive

_____   4. Emphasizes positive, yet doesn't "oversell"

_____   5. Spontaneous responses; no "canned" answers

_____   6. Expresses career goals and objectives

_____   7. Uses courteous language (please, thank you, etc.)

_____   8. No strong prejudices; tolerant of other's views; doesn't criticize others

_____   9. Checks understanding of questions with paraphrases

_____   10. Avoids yes/no answers; offers examples

Nonverbal Skills

_____   1. Shows enthusiasm

_____   2. Displays confidence, yet not arrogant

_____   3. Reveals maturity

_____   4. No nervous gestures

_____   5. No gum chewing

_____   6. Clean and conservative dress

_____   7. Good eye contact (not too much/little)

_____   8. Smiles from time to time

_____   9. Stands/sits straight/forward

_____   10. Speaks loudly and clearly

_____   TOTALS

Interview Rating Scale

80-72 = Hire at once
71-64 = Consider application
63-56 = Look for better candidate
55-48 = Not hire
47-down = Throw out of office

FOLLOW-UP LETTERS

After the interview, many applicants who have written letters of application, prepared a résumé, filled out application forms, and answered questions in an interview, think they have finished selling themselves to prospective employers. They fully believe that they have done their part to find a job.

In fact, most applicants share this belief. Unfortunately, the majority overlook a very important opportunity to follow-up on all the prior work they have done.

The "thanks-for-the-interview" letter may be the most important one they ever write, yet fewer than ten percent of applicants send one. The follow-up letter says a lot about you. It says, "I care"; "I am responsible"; "I'm better qualified than the other applicants for these specific reasons." It says, "I appreciate the time you spent with me, and I would like to work for your company."

This follow-up or thanks-for-the-interview letter provides another contact with the employer. It sets you apart from the countless applicants who don't take the time or initiative to write one. This extra effort on your part will certainly affect your standing in the eyes of the employer.

Several types of follow-up letters can be used. Some will simply thank the employer for the interview; others will express acceptance or rejection of a job offer. The content of these short letters should state your appreciation, explain what you liked about the position, and voice your enthusiasm about working for the firm.

These brief, to the point letters need not fill the page, but they should let the employer know you are grateful, regardless of the outcome of the interview. Notice in the following sample letters how the applicants express their thanks and interest in just a few short words.

Write a follow-up letter using the guidelines discussed. Thank the employer for an interview and express interest in the position.

Sample Follow-Up Letter 1

387 Apple Lane
Newtown, Illinois 61433
April 9, 1989

Mr. Bob Marks
Director of Personnel
ABC Travel, Incorporated
3287 Westgate Avenue
Chicago, Illinois 60619

Dear Mr. Marks:

It was a great pleasure to meet you yesterday and discuss with you my application for the position of travel agent with ABC Travel, Incorporated. I especially appreciated the opportunity to meet the other agents.

With my diploma in Travel Marketing and my strong organizational skills, I believe I would be an asset to your firm.

I appreciate your consideration and look forward to hearing from you.

Sincerely,

Jo Morgan

Sample Follow-Up Letter 2

903 Palm Drive
Miami, Florida 23984
June 28, 1989

Ms. Sandra Melendez
Director of Employment
Ace Corporation
11274 Orange Grove Road
Fort Lauderdale, Florida 24321

Dear Ms. Melendez:

Thank you for offering me the position of material handling technician at the Ace Corporation. I was impressed with the organization of your department and its commitment
to quality robotic repair.

Unfortunately, due to my conflicting schedule at school, I am unable to accept the
position at this time.

As you suggested, I will contact you when I finish my robotics training. If another
position should occur that you think would fit my schedule before completion of my
training, please feel free to contact me at (305) 783-9730.

Sincerely,

Carroll Rowe

Step 4: Maintaining Employment Satisfaction

Once you have obtained your desired position, you will want to keep it and realize the satisfaction of performing your job well. We believe that the skills which will help you keep your position are the sending and receiving skills that we have developed throughout this text.

However, certain attitudes must accompany these skills and are reflected in their use. These include, but are not limited to, the following:

1. *Enthusiastic*—eager to work and learn new aspects of the job; doing things without having to be asked; putting forth your best effort.
2. *Cooperative*—working well with customers, co-workers, supervisors; respectful of others; adaptable to changes in working conditions and schedules.
3. *Honest*—not stealing equipment or supplies; following company policies and procedures; making the best use of your time while on the job.
4. *Dependable*—getting to work on time; completing assigned work on schedule and in a responsible way; proper maintenance of tools and equipment.

Success in maintaining employment depends on your ability to use the skills you have learned. Remember the following guidelines as you continue your communication for the world of work.

1. When you listen, notice the feelings as well as the content of the message. Listen to fully understand the other person.
2. When you respond, treat the sender with respect. Show that you value the person—and mean it!
3. When you assert yourself, be specific about your wants, needs, and feelings. Seek to meet your needs without violating the other's rights.
4. When you assume a leadership role, use your sending skills to clearly explain technical information to customers or new employees.
5. When you prepare any written communication, be guided by the principles of accuracy, clarity, and economy.
6. When the time comes to make an occupation or career change, use your employability skills to sell yourself and, your experience.

In conclusion, the whole employment process is akin to progressing on a game board (see example on page 190). In the job hunt "game," winning results in employment satisfaction, and losing results in the frustration of underemployment or even unemployment. Study and familiarize yourself with these steps, and go through all the minor and major activities if you wish to be fully satisfied in your career choice.

It is essential to remember that no one owes you a job because you've earned a degree. Finding work is, in fact, work itself. Securing a job that is satisfying requires your sincere and dedicated efforts. In the end, you will be well-rewarded with greater personal and job satisfaction.

On the job and in your personal life, you will need to develop the communication skills we have discussed in order to be successful. Now you need to develop the blueprint for continued improvement by incorporating them into your work and personal life.

These techniques will make you a valued employee, a good friend, and a respected family member. As your work can affect your personal life and vice

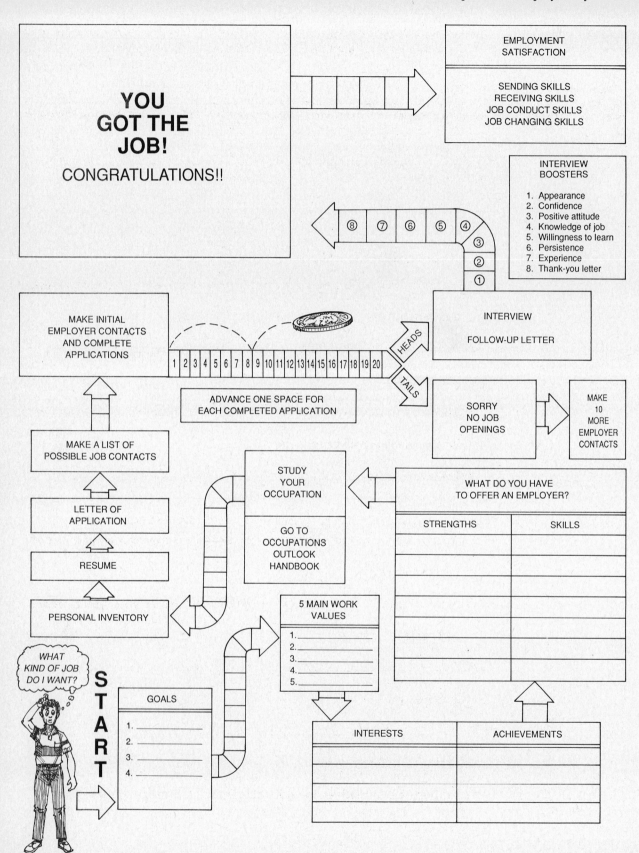

YOU
GOT THE
JOB!
CONGRATULATIONS!!

EMPLOYMENT
SATISFACTION

SENDING SKILLS
RECEIVING SKILLS
JOB CONDUCT SKILLS
JOB CHANGING SKILLS

INTERVIEW
BOOSTERS

1. Appearance
2. Confidence
3. Positive attitude
4. Knowledge of job
5. Willingness to learn
6. Persistence
7. Experience
8. Thank-you letter

⑧ ⑦ ⑥ ⑤ ④ ③ ② ①

MAKE INITIAL
EMPLOYER CONTACTS
AND COMPLETE
APPLICATIONS

INTERVIEW

FOLLOW-UP LETTER

HEADS   TAILS

1 2 3 4 5 6 7 8 9 10 11 12 13 14 15 16 17 18 19 20

ADVANCE ONE SPACE FOR
EACH COMPLETED APPLICATION

SORRY
NO JOB
OPENINGS

MAKE
10
MORE
EMPLOYER
CONTACTS

MAKE A LIST OF
POSSIBLE JOB CONTACTS

STUDY
YOUR
OCCUPATION

GO TO
OCCUPATIONS
OUTLOOK
HANDBOOK

WHAT DO YOU HAVE
TO OFFER AN EMPLOYER?

STRENGTHS	SKILLS

LETTER OF
APPLICATION

RESUME

PERSONAL INVENTORY

5 MAIN WORK
VALUES

1. _____
2. _____
3. _____
4. _____
5. _____

WHAT
KIND OF JOB
DO I WANT?

S
T
A
R
T

GOALS

1. _____
2. _____
3. _____
4. _____

INTERESTS	ACHIEVEMENTS

versa, you will realize that effective interpersonal communication is a key tool for your success and happiness in life and in the world of work.

CHAPTER 5 CHECK UP

Use these key words from the preceding chapter to complete the following sentences.

career	dependable	realistic
job	résumé	clerical
honest	enthusiastic	realistic
Occupational Outlook Handbook	letter of application	

1. An individual who prefers to fix things and use athletic or mechanical ability would be categorized as _____.

2. A_____ is defined as one's exact title, duties, and location of employment.

3. Your best source for obtaining information about various occupations and employment possibilities is the_____.

4. Following company policy is an indication that you are an_____ employee.

5. A_____ individual enjoys working with information and following instructions.

6. A_____ is a one- or two-page summary of your qualifications and skills.

7. A_____ is usually sent with your résumé and introduces you to an employer.

8. Being_____ means being responsible by completing your work duties on a timely basis.

9. Taking the initiative to do things and to learn shows you are _____.

10. Your general profession, which is usually seen as a lifelong pursuit, is called a_____.